2/83

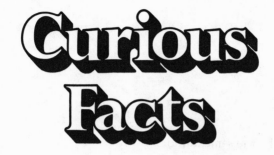

Curious Facts

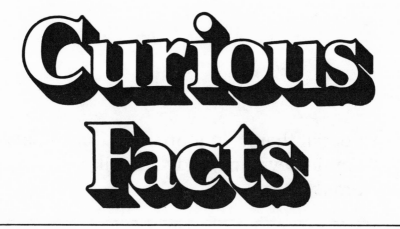

Curious Facts

JOHN MAY

with

Michael Marten   **David Brittain**
John Chesterman   **Lee Torrey**

Holt, Rinehart and Winston
New York

Special thanks to John Trux, Tanya Seton, Annie Leymarie, Judy Karasik, and David Smith

---

Copyright © 1980 by Clanose Publishers, Ltd.
All rights reserved, including the right to reproduce this book or portions thereof in any form.

First published in January 1981 by Holt, Rinehart and Winston, 383 Madison Avenue, New York, New York 10017.

Library of Congress Cataloging in Publication Data

May, John, 1950–
  Curious facts.

  Includes index.
  1. Curiosities and wonders. I. Title.
AG243.M36   031'.02   80-12123
ISBN Hardbound: 0-03-046776-4
ISBN Paperback: 0-03-046771-3

First Edition

Designer: Constance T. Doyle

Printed in the United States of America

10 9 8 7 6 5 4 3 2 1

"Experience has shown, and a true philosophy will always show, that a vast, perhaps the larger, portion of the truth arises from the seemingly irrelevant."

—Edgar Allan Poe

CONTENTS

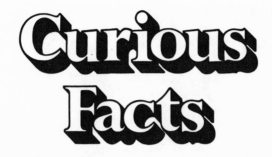

Curious Facts

INTRODUCTION

When asked to quote a curious fact, I usually relate a story that appeared in the December, 1975, issue of *National Geographic* in an article on the Maya civilization.

Author Howard La Fay recounts how, in the company of two professors, he descended the long stairway into the Temple of Inscriptions, the huge pyramidal tomb of Pacal, illustrious ruler of the city-state of Palenque. Inside the burial chamber the two professors were studying the various glyphs and symbols on the massive five-tone sarcophagus lid when they noticed that Pacal's left foot had a split in the big toe.

One of them claimed it must be a slip of the sculptor's chisel, but after close study Dr. Kelley cried, "No, It's not a mistake! That's a split toe, a congenital defect. I have it myself." He then pulled off shoe and sock to reveal his own toe, suffering from an identical split.

Curiosity is defined by Isaac Asimov as "the desire to know." The process whereby people lose interest in the world around them, on the other hand, is described by Lionel McColvin, in *How To Find Out*, as "the decay of curiosity." *Curious Facts* is stimulated by the first sentiment and designed to allay the second.

Our title comes from a small, battered volume bought from a junk stall in London's Portobello Road and originally published in the late nineteenth century. Entitled *Everybody's Scrapbook of Curious Facts*, it is a mine of information on such unlikely topics as Greasing Soldiers' Feet and Carving on Peach Stones.

Inspiration also came from the famous Potter's Museum of Curiosity at Arundel, in Sussex, which contains an extraordinary collection of miscellaneous objects, arranged in a haphazard jumble.

An albino hawfinch stands next to a blowpipe from the Solomon Islands and a lamb with two heads.

One showcase contains a mummy's head, a plume from King Victor Emmanuel's hat, lace bobbins, a dumdum bullet, and a Roman horseshoe.

A pair of white, wrinkled, Siamese-twin piglets stare mournfully from their bath of formaldehyde.

Curious Facts is designed to entertain in similar fashion, combining a mixture of stimulating information, unusual comparisons, queer coincidences, and strange stories in a style lying somewhere between Barnum and Borges—showmanship and erudition.

The tradition of collecting what many would dismiss as trivial information is long and distinguished. One of the great collectors of this century was Charles Fort, who spent a large part of his life poring over library archives and shuffling shoeboxes stuffed with newspaper clippings, then worked his raw data into a new world view which he expounded in rich, unexpected prose. He was fascinated by phenomena like falls of frogs and mass panics, teleportation and projected thought-forms, which challenged conventional scientific thought because they just didn't fit.

Fort attempted to weld all this scattered weirdness into a number of larger patterns. As he explained in one of his books, *Lo!*: "Wise men have tried to understand our state of being, by grasping at its stars, or its arts, or its economics. But, if there is an underlying oneness of all things, it does not matter where we begin, whether with stars, or laws of supply and demand, or frogs, or Napoleon Bonaparte. One measures a circle beginning anywhere."

A curious-fact collector of a different kind was Robert L. Ripley, world-famous originator of *Believe It or Not!* His snappy merging of words and pictures started an industry which still continues long after his death.

Ripley, in the introduction to the collected volumes of his work, wrote: "I make my living out of the fact that truth is stranger than fiction." He traveled extensively, viewing the curious nature of reality, and received up to one million letters a year from all over the world. "Despite the excessive demands from newspapers, cinemas, and broadcasts," he said, "the supply of *Believe It or Not!*

material remains inexhaustible. Each day it becomes easier to obtain."

Our own work in this area dates back some six years to when our group was formed to produce a new kind of encyclopedia called *An Index of Possibilities* (Wildwood House/Pantheon Books, 1974), whose aim was to emphasize the connections between subjects rather than what separated them. We felt that in this age of specialization it was increasingly difficult and increasingly important to gain a general knowledge of the world. One reviewer suggested our motto should be "Only Connect."

Our next book, *Worlds Within Worlds—A Journey into the Unknown* (Secker & Warburg/Holt, Rinehart and Winston, 1977), explored the new images of scientific photography, and the way in which their combination of information and aesthetics bridged the so-called gap between art and science.

Throughout these years we had been accumulating unusual information that didn't readily fit into any neat category, but which became impossible to throw away. The book you now hold in your hands originated from a small, scrappy "Amazing Facts" file which we kept on old computer cards.

Our approach has been to try to re-create the form of a Victorian book, using modern information. No limit was set on subject matter, though certain strong favorites emerged. The biggest problem came in trying to fit all the pieces together—the problem of classification.

In an article entitled "Variations on a Theme" in the *New Sci entist* (1974), Dr. Nick Humphrey argued that classification is an essential animal activity, a means of seeking out relevant information so as to enhance survival.

"An effective classification system," he wrote, "divides the world up in such a way that the objects in any one class, though they may differ in detail, share essential features which give them a common significance for the animal. Such a system reduces the thought load in the animal, expedites new learning, and allows rapid extrapolation from one set of circumstances to another."

In an era of information explosion, classification becomes ever more problematic. It is a dilemma that has been expressed eloquently by another curious-fact collector, Ivan T. Sanderson, founder of the Society for the Investigation of the Unexplained (SITU).

"While things and individual facts become ever more pattern-ized and thus classifiable," he says, "knowledge as a whole is becoming ever more muddled and, at the same time, ever more specialized. The more facts we accumulate and the better insight we gain into reality, the more they link up, so that it is becoming increasingly difficult to describe just where to lodge any particular item."

Unusual classification systems destroy traditional patterns of thought, forcing us to reexamine our assumptions. A classic exam-ple of this is quoted in the preface to *The Order of Things* (1970) by French philosopher Michel Foucault. It comes from the blind cosmic librarian Jorge Luis Borges, who quotes a certain Chinese encyclopedia in which it is written that:

"Animals are divided into: a) belonging to the Emperor, b) embalmed, c) tame, d) sucking pigs, e) sirens, f) fabulous, g) stray dogs, h) included in the present classification, i) frenzied, j) innu-merable, k) drawn with a very fine camel-hair brush, l) etcetera, m) having just broken the water pitcher, n) that from a long way off look like flies."

Foucault read this and his book "grew out of the laughter that shattered ... all the familiar landmarks of my thought—our thought that bears the stamp of our age and our geography—breaking up all the ordered surfaces and all the planes with which we are accustomed to tame the wild profusion of existing things."

We hope that our volume can produce the same laughter and disturbing thoughts. The alphabetical arrangement is merely a strap. The cross-referenced index allows you to enter the book from a number of directions and for a wide variety of reasons.

As Marshall McLuhan said of Expo '67: "It was just a mosaic of discontinuous items in which people took an immense satisfaction precisely *because* they weren't being told anything about the over-all pattern or shape of it, but they were free to discover and par-ticipate and involve themselves in the total overall thing. The result was also that they never got fatigued."

John May
Bourton-on-the-Water
January 14, 1979

ACRONYMS

Sheep in the mountains of North Wales have been fitted with electronic "bleep" devices so that farmers can trace their movements across the rugged terrain. The device has been christened BO-PEEP: Bangor Orange Position Estimating Equipment for Pastures.

Acronyms have proliferated so rapidly that you can now get dictionaries of them. A 757-page American directory contains this gem: ADCOMAMPHIBFORPACFLOOM. That stands for Administrative Command, Amphibious Forces, Pacific Fleet (Subordinate Command).

Another place they are having acronym trouble is at ESA (European Space Agency). If you ask them what a MOG is, you'll be informed politely that it's a MIEC Operator Guide. And a MIEC? That's the Meteorological Information Extraction Center. MIEC is also heavily involved in FGGE, the First Global GARP experiment. GARP is, of course, the Global Atmospheric Research Program. What you really need at ESA is a DEACON: the Definitions, Abbreviations, and Conventions handbook.

One of the major problems in immunology research is how the body creates such an enormous variety of antibodies. This question is popularly known in research labs as the GOD problem. GOD is the Generator of Diversity.

Methane gas derived from cow manure is fueling gas cookers in 3,500 Chicago homes. The system is run by the Calorific Recovery Anaerobic Process Inc., popularly known by its acronym—CRAP.

ACTORS AND ACTRESSES

Bob Hope once tried a career in amateur boxing under the name Packy Ease.

Rock Hudson was originally called Roy Fitzgerald. He got his new name from his agent Henry Wilson, who claimed: "I named him after the Rock of Gibraltar and the Hudson River."

Theda Bara was originally Theodosia Goodman from Cincinnati; her new name was an anagram of Arab Death.

W. C. Fields was so afraid of losing his loose cash that he used to open bank accounts whenever he found himself with loose money in his pocket. Among the pseudonyms he used were: Figley E. Whitesides, Aristotle Hoop, Ludovic Fishpond, and Cholmondley Frampton-Blythe.

Hundreds of these accounts are still open all over the country. Fields never made a master list, so many of them will never be closed out.

When Lucille Ball was under contract to MGM, she was loaned to Paramount for a De Mille picture, *The Greatest Show on Earth*, but then discovered she was pregnant. De Mille told husband Desi Arnaz: "Congratulations. You're the only man who's ever screwed his wife, Cecil B. De Mille, Paramount Pictures, and Harry Cohn all at the same time."

Humphrey Bogart once said: "In my first twenty-nine pictures, I was shot in twelve, electrocuted or hanged in eight, and was a jailbird in nine. Is that a record to be proud of?"

That is not James Dean's voice you hear in the drunken banquet scene in *Giant*. The voice belongs to actor Nick Adams, who was paid $300 for three days' dubbing. This was necessary because Dean's mumbling was inaudible and when it came time to redub, Dean was already dead and buried.

Peter Finch, the only actor to win an Oscar posthumously, was the son of physicist Professor George Finch, who was a mountaineer on the 1922 Leigh-Mallory expedition to Mt. Everest.

Horror movie stars Peter Cushing, Vincent Price, and Christopher Lee were all born on May 27.

Barber Kelly Russo added Rudolph Valentino's "destiny ring" to his collection of Valentino mementoes, even though a curse was alleged to befall the owner. Valentino, who died wearing the cat's-eye ring, is said to have purchased it in a San Francisco novelty store. The major Hollywood studios' chosen successor to Valentino, Russ Columbo, fell heir to the ring and subsequently died in a car accident while wearing it, shortly before shooting his first movie. Next came Joe Casino, a close friend of Columbo's; he died when a truck hit him. The ring was won by Russo when Casino's brother held a competition to be rid of it.

Pablo Picasso wrote a play called *Desire Caught by the Tail* starring Jean-Paul Sartre and Simone de Beauvoir, which was such a miserable failure that it has only been performed three times since 1941. Its characters—Fat Anxiety, Big Foot, and Thin Anguish—caused one pained critic to write that the play combined "the features of medieval morality plays with twentieth-century smut."

ADVERTISING

De l'Isle-Adam's *Cruel Tales,* published in 1883, contains a story, "Celestial Publicity," in which the night sky is used for advertising. He writes:
"A moment's reflection is enough to allow one to imagine the consequences of this ingenious invention. Would not the Great Bear herself have cause for astonishment if, between her sublime paws, there suddenly appeared this disquieting question: 'Are corsets necessary?'"

Like their modern counterparts, many silent-screen stars endorsed products and appeared in advertisements. Anna Q. Nilsson appeared in ads for twenty different products, including shampoo, shoe polish, razors, toothpaste, and railroads.

Tom Mix endorsed a health ray, Rudolph Valentino a beauty clay, Corinne Griffith a vibrator, and Dolores del Rio endorsed California lemons.

Advertising on American TV for the 1978 Super Bowl cost $325,000 per minute, the highest such price in history.

Subliminal advertising was invented by Jim Vicary, an American market researcher, who arranged with the owner of a New Jersey cinema to install a second projector. While the main feature was running, Vicary flashed slogans like "Eat popcorn" and "Coca-Cola" on the screen, an experiment he conducted on alternate evenings. The messages had the effect of boosting Coke sales by one-sixth, popcorn by over a half.

At an advertising symposium at Atlantic City in 1923, one aphorism delivered to the audience read: "Appeal to reason in your advertising, and you appeal to four percent of the human race."

ALCOHOL – THE DEMON DRINK

Alcoholics Anonymous was founded by Bill Wilson and Dr. Bob Smith, who first met in the Akron City Hospital.

Wilson at one time corresponded with Carl Jung; both agreed that an alcoholic's craving was, in some ways, a low-level equivalent of the mystic's need for spiritual experience.

Paul Ricard, the French aperitif millionaire, who made his fortune selling *pastis*, a pale anise spirit, was famous for his extravagent stunts. Once he took his entire staff of fifteen hundred to Rome to receive Pope John XXIII's blessing.

The Pier Hotel, Port Headland, Australia, is claimed to be one of the toughest pubs in the world, and one of the most profitable, with a turnover of more than $2 million a year. Every day they sell 6,000 glasses of beer—some 140 gallons. Breakages run at 90 glasses a day or 3,300 a year. (One favorite drink is Tia Maria and Coke, which costs $20 a quart jug.)

In New Delhi an average of three thousand Indians die every year from drinking poisonous homemade alcohol or "hootch." One stock analyzed by official chemists revealed traces of lye, paint thinner, antifreeze, dead rats, snakes, dogs, fertilizers, and swamp water.

The expression "the real McCoy" came from Bill McCoy, who was a rumrunner to the United States from the British West Indies, whose reputation was that he supplied his customers with the best booze in the world.

In 1950, it took a British male manual worker twenty-three minutes to earn enough for a pint of beer, and eleven hours to earn enough for a bottle of whiskey.

By 1976, these times had been reduced to twelve minutes and three and a half hours respectively.

Russians call vodka "a little ray of sunshine in the stomach." The official state term for alcoholics is "partial suicides."

There are cows in County Cork, Ireland, which produce a bottle of gin a day—seriously. The largest plant manufacturing Irish cheddar cheese has discovered a use for the waste product of the process, a watery liquid called *whey*. The solid matter suspended in this is being treated to produce the alcohol base used by gin distilleries. Similar experiments are being carried out in the Netherlands. Claims Dutch chemist Dr. Frans Nieuwenhof: "The average cow gives about 1,250 gallons of milk every year. This is enough to produce about two hundred bottles of whiskey or gin."

The Germans more or less reverse the process. In Bavaria, beef cattle are fed on *sclempe*, a kind of high-protein sludge which is a by-product of the manufacture of schnapps, and is often piped directly from the distillery to the feeding trough.

Another form of alcoholic recycling was suggested by British scientist Dr. Gerald Griffin, during an address to the American Chemical Society convention in Miami, when he proposed that hops could be used to build the bars as well as brew the beer. He explained how it would be possible to make building board from spent hops, or even use them as resins in paint. The plants appear to be as versatile as Indian hemp.

Ethyl alcohol molecules have been discovered in a huge gas cloud in interstellar space by Dr. Benjamin Zuckerman of the University of Maryland. According to Zuckerman, "preliminary estimates indicate that the alcohol content of this cloud, if purged of all impurities and condensed, would yield 10^{28} fifths at two hundred proof."

This exceeds the total amount of all humanity's fermentation efforts since the beginning of recorded time.

Thirty-six laboratory rats at the University of California were housed in a "condominium," fitted with individual burrows and a common living area, and complete with a bar consisting of three spigots dispensing plain water and three dispensing a ten-percent solution of alcohol flavored with anise.

The rats took to the taps with glee. At first they would spend a "happy hour" socializing and drinking before their food arrived, then they began to take a quick nightcap before retiring to their burrows. The colony's alcohol consumption rose steadily until finally the rats began indulging in day-long binges. For several days afterwards they exhibited symptoms of hangovers—diminished alcohol intake, increased water intake.

AMPHETAMINES

Amphetamine improves the ability of monkeys to read facial expressions.

A special report published in 1971 by the U.S. Select Committee on Crime revealed that in the four years 1966–1969, the U.S. Army consumed more amphetamines than did the entire British and American armed forces during World War II. In total, the official U.S. military issue of amphetamines during this period came to well over 225 million standard-dose tablets.

In order to demonstrate how easy it was to obtain stimulants in large quantities from drug companies, a CBS news producer named Jay McCullen rented an office and a post office box in Manhattan. He then set himself up as a bogus import-export firm—McCullen Services.

Simply by writing to nine drug companies and suppliers on paper imprinted with his letterhead, McCullen obtained more than one million amphetamine and barbiturate pills and capsules worth over $500,000 on the black market—for an outlay of just six hundred dollars.

The first form of amphetamine to be introduced on the market was the benzedrine inhaler. This became so popular that in 1946 it was immortalized in a hit song, "Who Put the Benzedrine in Mrs. Murphy's Ovaltine?," a parody of "Who Put the Overalls in Mrs. Murphy's Chowder?"

ANTIQUE AIR

In order to test whether or not the Earth's atmosphere had been affected by fluorocarbons, scientists at Washington State University had to locate "antique air" in old, unopened tin cans or sunken wrecks in order to have a test sample.

ANTS

Ants are the most numerically abundant of social insects. At any given moment there are at least 10^{15} (or 1,000,000,-000,000,000) living ants on the earth.

Fire ants infest more than 130 million acres in the southern United States, including two-thirds of the state of Georgia. In parts of Mississippi there are as many as two hundred fire ant mounds per acre.

Fire ants dig their stingers into a victim's flesh and hold on for up to twenty-five seconds, driving their toxic venom into the bloodstream. Stings often lead to bacterial infection because the venom prevents the white blood cells from reaching the skin around the stings.

In 1973, a retired railroad brakeman from Texas died several months after multiple bites in his leg—despite amputation of the afflicted limb.

Edmund O. Wilson, author of *The Insect Societies*, described a driver ant colony as a single "animal" weighing in excess of twenty kilograms and possessing on the order of twenty million mouths.

One of the world's biggest red ant colonies has been found by scientists in a forest in the Jura Mountains. An estimated three hundred million ants live there in twelve hundred anthills, each two meters high, which are linked by miniature highways.

APHRODISIACS

In Georgian England, favorite aphrodisiacs included tongues of guinea fowl, extract from the sinews in the tentacles of an octopus, the brains of doves, and the testes of all animals, especially the lion.

According to an enterprising promoter in the Indian village of Takayanagi, snakes have aphrodisiac qualities. He sells to tourists a "mashumi burger," which contains two-thirds of a small poisonous snake. To eat the whole snake, he claims, would drive a person to sexual frenzy.

Cantherides, or Spanish fly, is a drug with reputed aphrodisiacal powers, extracted from a small beetle common in Central and Southern Europe. The sixteenth-century physician Cabrol reported a case in Provence where some women fed their husbands Spanish fly to cure them of "the fever." One woman claimed that in two nights her husband made love to her eighty-seven times and then became ill. He made it three more times during the medical examination, and then, after gangrene had begun to attack his penis, died.

Japanese farmers have produced a liquor that is supposed to add zest to sex. The drink tastes of apples and is flavored with dead earthworms.

APPARITIONS

According to a spokesman for the Oxford-based Institute for Psychophysical Research: "Apparitions in West Africa seem to behave quite normally, more like real people. One letter (we received) told of a person who appeared and went about his daily business quite normally—and only after a few days did somebody realize that the person had been dead for some time."

The "motorway legend" is a modern fairy tale, here related by Mrs. Newall of the British Folklore Society:
"It's a tale of a phantom hitchhiker. A young man on the motorway picks up a girl who is shivering with cold. He lends her his sweater and drops her at her home. A few days later, he stops at the house to call for his sweater, only to learn that the girl was killed in a traffic accident months before. Going back to where he picked her up, he sees a cemetery where his sweater is found draped over her tomb."

ARMS, LEGS, AND FEET

In 1978, the Goodyear Rubber Company reported that decades of research at its Windsor, Vermont, testing facility had led to the incontrovertible conclusion that shoes on right feet wear out faster than shoes on left feet.

Professional basketball player Clifford Ray of California's Golden State Warriors was called in to help retrieve a piece of metal from the stomach of a 350-pound dolphin. Only his three-foot, nine-inch-long arms could reach it.

Guy Noel, who has no legs, holds an endurance record for swimming two hundred hours in a canal at Calais.

Police in Winchester, England, received an emergency call from a man whose wife was holding him against his will by hiding his artificial leg.

Soldiers with flat feet are no longer banned from frontline duty in the Israeli army.

AROUND THE WORLD

Lieutenant Colonel Sigmund Jahn of East Germany worked out on a fixed training bicycle machine while orbiting Earth in Russia's Salyut 6 space station. In the process he became the first man to cycle nonstop around the world.

Dave Kunst walked around the world in four and a half years, covering a distance of fifteen thousand miles and wearing out twenty-one pairs of shoes. During the journey he was seriously wounded when his brother John was shot to death by Afghan bandits thirty months after the beginning of the journey. Dave returned to the U.S. to recuperate and then, undeterred, set off again from Afghanistan with Peter, his younger brother—accompanied by forty armed Afghan government guards.

Unable to get permission to cross China by foot, the brothers took a ship to Australia where they walked across that continent—equal to the distance across China. The final leg of the journey was from Newport Beach, California, to Minnesota, where Dave arrived on October 5, 1974.

ARSON

Merill Klein was a professional arsonist or "torch" for more than a decade, during which time he planned or started fires that caused damage amounting to millions of dollars.

On one occasion he burned down a Kentucky bakery, first making sure the sprinkler system was out of operation by freezing it with dry ice. He added considerably to his profit by filling the bakery with scrap plastic he'd bought for virtually nothing, and then claimed on his insurance premium that the building was a thriving plastics factory.

A nineteen-year-old Australian navy seaman was found guilty of destroying twelve Australian navy planes when he tossed a burning paper airplane into a crowded hangar.

In 1968, a British Fire Research Station statistical study revealed that the average arsonist was a male teenager, most likely to strike seven days after the new moon.

ART

The Museum of Modern Art in New York hung *Le Bateau* by Matisse upside-down for forty-seven days before they discovered their mistake.

American artist Ed Kienholtz started "trade in art" by printing the name of an object he required on luxury paper and signing it with his thumbprint. It was a modest beginning, with a request for nine screwdrivers, which advanced rapidly to fur coats, Browning automatics, legal expenses, and finally dollars. When he decides to call it a day, he intends to have an X cut into his thumb by a plastic surgeon, thereby canceling it as a printing device and so protecting the investor. The surgery has been paid for in advance on the usual trade-in-art terms.

Art Morrison, a leading figure in American Midwest Farm Art, produces hundreds of identical fourteen-inch-high ceramic chickens he calls Juxtapachickens. One of his Corn Corners Farm Art events, a conceptual piece entitled *Portable Pig Pulley*, involved hoisting a feeding pig by means of pulleys to test the theory that the animal would digest its fodder more quickly in that position.

Media Burn, an event performed by a group of American artists called Ant Farm, consisted of two "media artists," one a John F. Kennedy look-alike, driving a metallic silver "dream car," with a hood fifteen feet long and a huge dorsal fin, through a wall of burning television sets in a San Francisco parking lot on July 4, 1975. The whole event was recorded by video camera.

Body artist Dennis Oppenheim lay in the sun for hours, unprotected except for an open book which he had placed facedown on his chest. The resulting artwork, a photograph entitled *Reading Position for a Second Degree Burn* (1970), revealed the artist's severely burned skin, surrounding an untouched rectangle of flesh on his chest.

Lead Sink for Sebastian was another 1970 piece, this one involving an amputee whose left leg was fitted with a surrogate lead "limb." A butane blowtorch attached to his right ankle slowly melted the lead limb until his body became lopsided.

In 1971, Oppenheim's *Fear* found the artist standing stationary within a five-and-a-half-foot-diameter circle while people lobbed rocks at him. A video camera recorded his facial expressions.

In 1972, Oppenheim reproduced two attempts to jump across a creek in Idaho, this time in a New York gallery. Oppenheim jumped on wet plaster which set his footmarks for posterity. The piece was entitled *Dead Dog Creek*.

Sculptor Carl Andre's *American Decay* (1973) opened at the Preteth Gallery, Washington, on January 19—and closed the following day because of the putrid smell. The sculpture consisted of five hundred pounds of cottage cheese anointed with ten gallons of ketchup atop tarpaper covering an area of twelve feet by eighteen feet. The cheese itself was ten inches deep.

ASSAULT AND BATTERY

A nineteen-year-old seaman in the U.S. Navy was sentenced to six months in the brig, demotion in rank, and a $400 fine for smacking a commanding officer in the face with a chocolate cream pie—this despite the fact that, during his trial, expert evidence was given by TV comic Soupy Sales, who said that in his experience of receiving 19,253 pies in the face, it did not amount to assault.

In 1975, an ultra-rightist in Tokyo got two years at hard labor for slapping Premier Takeo Miki in the face. The judge said he had "insulted Miki and the people and greatly impaired Japan's international prestige."

In 1976, a twenty-four-year-old man in Tulsa, Oklahoma, was convicted of assault and fined two hundred dollars for kissing a policewoman's elbow while she attempted to give him a parking ticket.

ASTONISHING SURVIVALS

Nineteen-year-old Gene Lewis of Long Island was helping his local bar manager with a couple of rowdies when one of them pulled out a .32-caliber revolver, held it against Lewis's throat, and pulled the trigger twice. The gun failed to go off. He then put it into Lewis's mouth and pulled the trigger again. The gun failed again. Police later confirmed that it was fully loaded.

In 1960, a Russian tractor driver named Vladimir Khami got lost in a snowstorm and was discovered after being buried under snow for three hours. His body was blue and stiff, but without any sign of frostbite or putrefaction. Khami, after he recovered in the hospital, said he had become unconscious after inhaling the carbon dioxide from his own breath.

Peter Johnson, twenty-three, a candy salesman from Kent, won a thirty-minute battle for his life when his car landed upside down in five feet of water. It took him ten minutes to force his way into the car's trunk, five minutes to clear away his samples and find a wrench, and fifteen minutes of hammering before the lock gave way, leaving him enough room to squeeze out to the surface. Said Johnson: "It was really the halfpenny which saved my life. It was the only coin I had in my pocket and I used it to unscrew the back seat to get into the boot. . . . As I worked on the screws I could feel the water collecting underneath me on the roof. I worked away at the lock of the boot. . . . It was the only chance I had. Finally it gave, but as soon as I moved the boot lid, the water and mud gushed in."

Army sergeant Robert Herd, forty-seven, fell eleven hundred feet when his parachute failed to open over West Virginia and his reserve chute got entangled. He landed on his feet, rolled onto his back, and suffered only a cracked vertebra.

Eighteen-month-old baby Matthew Williams was knocked down and run over by a car in Worcestershire, England. One of the car's wheels rolled directly over his stomach. But Matthew was quite unaffected by the incident. To the bafflement of doctors, he wasn't even bruised.

A swimmer surfaced in Washington State's Skokomish river after spending four hours unconscious in a freak air pocket under a rock.

Yugoslav bus driver Hamdija Osman, thirty-four, was lying under his crowded vehicle trying to repair a brake, when the bus started rolling slowly toward the edge of a four-hundred-foot precipice.

Osman jammed his left leg under the nearest wheel in a bid to stop it, but it merely rolled straight over and broke his leg in four places. In spite of his pain, Osman jammed his right leg under the other wheel—and the bus stopped on the brink of the cliff, saving the lives of the thirty passengers on board.

AVALANCHES

Scientists divide avalanches into three main types:

1.) Those consisting of dry, powdery snow, which move at speeds of up to two hundred miles an hour and are preceded by a shock wave forceful enough to demolish buildings and snap tree trunks even before the snow arrives, and in which the extremely fine snow crystals can penetrate the lungs and suffocate anyone in the avalanche's path.

2.) Those consisting of wet, sludgy snow, which move at only about twenty miles an hour but exert a pressure of up to several tons per square foot.

3.) "Slab" avalanches, the most dangerous of all, where a whole mountain slope's snow cover begins to break up and move ponderously down to engulf anything in its way.

BAT BOMB

About thirty million bats were rounded up by the U.S. Army Air Corps in 1943, with the intention of developing a bat bomb.

The idea was to attach to each bat a device weighing one ounce that produced a flame on a delay fuse. They then planned to release the bats over enemy cities, where it was hoped that they would fly into attics and under eaves and await ignition.

Following an investment of two million dollars, the bats were declared operational in 1945 but never used. In the United States, a general's car and a hangar were destroyed when some of the bats were accidentally released.

BEARS

Pliny the Elder believed that bears were born as tiny masses of unformed flesh and claws that the mother bear gradually licked into the shape of a cub.

All polar bears are left-handed; they never use their right paw in attack or defense. Fully grown, they can reach nine feet tall and weigh one thousand pounds. Polar bears' livers contain very high concentrations of Vitamin A, an overdose of which killed off all the members of a nineteenth-century Arctic expedition who ate the liver of one they'd killed.

Panda and koala bears are not bears at all. The panda is most closely related to the raccoon. The koala, a marsupial, is more closely related to the kangaroo.

A famous nineteenth-century bear was Tiglath-Pilesar, or "Tig" for short. A pet of one Frank Buckland, Tig was often seen wearing academic dress, was introduced to Florence Nightingale, hypnotized by Lord Houghton, and eventually confined to London Zoo when his behavior became too outrageous.

In the eighteenth century, bear grease was an accepted and well-known hair restorer. An advertisement in the *Daily Universal Register* proclaimed: "A. Little, Perfumer, No. 1 Portugal Street, Lincoln Inn Fields, acquaints the Public, that he has killed a remarkable fine Russian BEAR, the fat of which is matured by time to a proper state. He begs leave to solicit their attention to this Animal, which, for its fatness and size, is a real curiosity. He is now selling the fat, cut from the Animal, in boxes at 2s. 6d., and 5s. each, or rendered down in pts., from one shilling to One Guinea Each."

BEATING AND BATTERING

The Eton College *Chronicle* records that Dr. John Keats, the headmaster from 1809 to 1839, used his birch twigs a great deal. In 1818, the boys rioted and smashed his desk to pieces with sledgehammers, but Keats remained unconcerned and carried on teaching among the debris. The "greatest of them all," though, was Dr. Heath, who, on one occasion, flogged seventy boys, one after another. The result was that he "injured himself so badly that he was laid up with aches and pains for more than a week."

In 1977, a London city councilor discovered that the canes used to punish local schoolchildren were purchased from a sex bookshop that had been raided twice that year by the police. They were made by Ken Brown, an odd-job man, who had supplied the city's schools with four thousand in just three years.

Elderly Americans are suffering more and more beatings at the hands of their children, a university researcher told Congress in 1978. Professor Suzanne Steinmetz of the University of Delaware said: "The reported battering of parents with fists and objects to 'make them mind' or to change their minds about wills, financial management, or the signing of other papers is, unfortunately, a growing phenomenon."

BEES

Killer bees have been responsible for the deaths of between one hundred and three hundred persons in Brazil since 1957. In one incident in 1973, the inhabitants of the town of Recife were terrorized for hours by one swarm; it took asbestos-clad firemen with flamethrowers to disperse them.

It is the bees' method of constant attack which is more deadly than their sting. They sting up to sixty times a minute in a continual assault that can last for up to two hours. One person survived 2,243 stings, but 400 to 500 are generally fatal.

Beekeepers in England have been warned against placing their hives under high-voltage power lines. Scientists have discovered that bees constantly exposed to the wires' electrical field develop abnormal honey-producing patterns. A German zoologist who studied sixteen thousand bees in a high-tension field watched them kill their queen, then suffocate themselves by blocking the hive entrance with wax.

The largest known bee, the xylocopid or carpenter bee, is so determined to find a mate that it will try to seduce almost anything that flies. A biology professor who spent two years studying the bee's sexual habits claimed that males often mistook dandelion seeds, birds, and even aircraft for females of the species.

When a swarm of bees moves from one location to another, it constructs the cells of its new hive along exactly the same magnetic axis, demonstrating an incredible sensitivity to the Earth's magnetic field.

BICYCLES

The increase in the popularity of bicycling in the nineteenth century led to a decline in church attendance so pronounced that in 1896 a Baltimore preacher was led to deliver the following condemnation from the pulpit: "Those bladder-wheeled bicycles are diabolical devices of the demon of darkness. They are contrivances to trap the feet of the unwary and skin the nose of the innocent. They are full of guile and deceit. When you think you have broken one to ride and subdued its wild and Satanic nature, behold it bucketh you off in the road and teareth a great hole in your pants. Look not on the bike when it bloweth upon its wheels for at least it bucketh like a bronco and hurteth like thunder. Who has skinned legs? Who has a bloody nose? Who has ripped breeches? They that dally along with the bicycle."

BIONICS

A glance through recent developments in the replacement of human body parts reveals the following: plastic arteries molded from sea-urchin spines; artificial bones made from ceramics; plastic lenses inserted into the eyes of cataract victims; artificial hands electronically controlled by muscles in the patient's arm stump; metal and plastic ball-and-socket hip joints for arthritis sufferers; artificial knees made from noncorrosive chromium, nickel, and cobalt; artificial nerves made by the Russians from tantalum metal wire to treat a form of facial paralysis.

Engineers at the Westinghouse Corporation have developed a nuclear-powered bionic heart that costs $50,000 and, according to their spokesman: "will stand fire and impact should a heart recipient be involved in a crash of some sort, and the shielding material was built to stop a .38 slug."

BIRDS

Park-keepers report that male mallard ducks in London parks are suffering from "character collapse." Abandoning their wives and young, the drakes have taken to marauding in all-male gangs, bullying other wildlife, and molesting female mallards. They've also developed homosexual tendencies. Ornithologists blame tourists who feed the drakes—which have gorgeous plumage—in preference to the drabber female mallards.

A flamingo called Pedro in Banham Zoo near Norwich, England, was fitted with an artificial leg made of plastic tubing after breaking his own.

The great tit, a native British bird, defends his territory from other great tits by what has been dubbed the "Beau Geste effect." The bird has a repertory of four deterrent songs so that any intruder is deceived into thinking that several birds are already in possession of a particular territory and its food supplies.

Bird strikes are such a serious threat at many airports that all kinds of measures are used to deter them. Standard tactics involve the use of chemical repellents, scarecrows, and pop guns. But some airports have employed remote-controlled model planes shaped like hawks, or deployed airport officials to mime large birds of prey by flapping their arms and uttering menacing squawks.

In one of the most terrifying bird attacks on record, Italian glider pilot Antonio Beozzi fought a life-and-death battle with a golden eagle, 4,500 feet above the Alps. The bird swooped straight at the glider and crashed through the cabin cover. Said Beozzi: "The eagle tore at me. I felt its claws in my flesh. I fought back covered with blood." He managed to strangle the bird to death just as his craft dived out of control. He claimed later: "It was the ultimate fear."

The navigational abilities of birds are known to be extraordinary, but few can compare with the uncanny accuracy of a Manx shearwater, a type of seabird that was taken to Boston from its home in Wales. It flew the 4,800 kilometers back to its nest in just twelve days, arriving before the letter that announced its departure.

Flemish artist Roelandt Savery, the only painter who is believed to have sketched a live dodo bird (it became extinct in 1681), painted two right legs on the creature. It became the model for generations of copyists, who repeated the structural error.

The European swift feeds exclusively on flying insects and is believed to spend its whole life in the air, except when nesting. Finnish ornithologists have observed that at the approach of the summer cyclones from the North Atlantic, the birds leave well in advance of the storms and fly hundreds of miles to the south or north. They know that while a cyclone rages, their essential insect food is grounded. Meanwhile, their young, who have to be left in the nest, immediately hibernate until their parents return.

Crawford H. Greenewalt, president in the early 1950s of the powerful Du Pont Corporation, was fascinated by hummingbirds and determined to discover how fast they flew. With the aid of equipment built for him by high-speed photography pioneer Harold E. Edgerton, Greenewalt developed a device he nicknamed "Daddy's torture chamber." It consisted of an eighteen-inch pipe; air was driven down the pipe toward a feeder at the end. The birds would try to feed while Greenewalt altered the speed of the air current, an experiment he claimed they enjoyed tremendously. From this he calculated that hummingbirds fly at twenty-seven miles an hour.

BIRTHS ... AND HOW TO STOP THEM

The first recorded birth in Antarctica was on January 7, 1978, when a baby boy was delivered at an Argentinian army base.

Men and women of the Hua tribe of Papua, New Guinea, believe that men can become pregnant, and claim to have seen fetuses emerging from men's bodies.

They believe that men can become pregnant in three ways: first, by eating food that has been touched by a menstruating woman; second, by eating the opossum, which is a taboo food because the animal's fur is like pubic hair and because they believe that it leaps out of a tree like a baby from its mother; third, by sorcery.

Condoms were used in Rome but not rediscovered until eleven hundred years later by the Italian anatomist Gabriel Fallopius, who gave his name to the fallopian tube. His condom consisted of a linen sheath soaked in certain chemicals.

The "French letter" used to be called the "French bladder." Imported to England where they were in great demand for prevention of venereal disease, they consisted of a sheath made of the membrane from the stomach of a young sheep.

A Taiwanese actress gave birth on stage while performing in a harvest thanksgiving opera called *Little Dragon*. At first the audience thought it was a well-acted part of the plot.

A woman in Richmond, Virginia, has given birth to four consecutive sets of twins. The odds against this occurring are 65,610,000 to one. She had taken no fertility drugs and has five other children besides.

The earliest known reference to birth control is contained in an Egyptian papyrus of about 2000 B.C., which recommends application to the vagina of a bizarre mixture of crocodile excrement, honey, and soda.

The Danish word for contraceptive is *Svangerskabs-forebyggendemiddel.*

Alpine salamanders remain pregnant for more than three years and always give birth to twins.

BISEXUAL TROUT

Bisexual trout, which produce both eggs and sperm, have been bred at the French National Institute for Agronomical Research. The process involved feeding young normal trout with a chemical that affects their sex differentiation. Within two to three years, thirty percent become bisexual. Each bisexual trout can produce about one thousand normal, but genetically identical, baby trout. Researchers hope the technique will prove useful for quality control in fish farming.

BOARD GAMES

Board games certainly go back as far as 3000 B.C., the date of one dug out from the Royal Tombs of Ur by Sir Leonard Woolley. This used a twenty-square board with seven black and seven white counters, and is thought to have been an ancestor of backgammon. An unusual feature was that it was played with six pyramid-shaped dice.

The Mongol emperor Tamburlaine played Great Chess on a 110-square board. New pieces introduced included a Princess (combining the moves of Bishop and Knight), an Empress (Rook and Knight), and an Amazon (Queen and Knight).

In 1949, a Jordanian invented Atomic Chess. When a pawn reached the base line it became an atomic missile which could jump to any square to "blow up" any piece in its vicinity.

Every September in the Italian town of Marostica, the inhabitants play a game of living chess in the town's checkerboard square. The tradition dates back to 1454, when this method was used to decide which of two young noblemen should have the hand of the daughter of the local notable. Not every chess piece is a person; some are police horses.

Monopoly is the best-selling copyrighted game ever, with sales now past eighty million sets. Invented by Charles Darrow, an unemployed heating engineer from Philadelphia, it was eventually sold to Parker Brothers after they had initially turned it down in 1933, claiming that it contained "fifty-two fundamental playing errors." At the age of forty-seven, Darrow was able to retire a millionaire on the game's proceeds, and spent the rest of his life growing exotic orchids.

The street names on the American board came from Atlantic City. The Monopoly lobby successfully prevented the Atlantic City council from trying to change one of the community's street names.

The most expensive Monopoly set in the world was made by Alfred Dunhill and cost five thousand dollars.

An edible version of Monopoly, touted as a Christmas present with a difference, features a board, property cards, and player's symbols made of black chocolate, and hotels and houses made of milk chocolate or butterscotch. The price tag: six hundred dollars.

In 1975, the U.S. mint printed twenty-two billion dollars' worth of real money; in the same year, Parker Brothers printed forty billion dollars' worth of Monopoly money.

The Polish have a board game similar to Monopoly, called Directors. Played on a circular board, its object is to make as much money as possible—but for the factory, not for the individual.

One idea submitted to Waddingtons, the British manufacturers of Monopoly, was for a board game called Unemployment. It failed miserably.

BODY STONES

Mineral deposits can build up quite readily in various parts of the human body.

Gallstones, for instance, are composed of cholesterol, calcium salts, and bile pigments; they tend to have facets, like diamonds, because of the constant pressure and friction to which they are subjected in the gall bladder.

Kidney stones are formed from the crystallized constituents of urine and grow in laminated layers. Bladder stones, also known as *vesical calculi*, often look like coarse sand grains. Both Napoleon III of France and Leopold I of

Belgium suffered from this condition, which makes urinating very painful. In some cases bladder stones grow around a foreign object trapped in the bladder. A twin-lobed stone extracted from a twenty-nine-year-old man was built around an open tie pin, while another specimen taken from a seventeen-year-old contained a still-intact pea which the boy had introduced into his urethra, or urine duct, fourteen months previously.

BOGUS PATIENTS

Bogus patients are known to doctors as "Munchhausens" after Baron Hieronymous Karl Friedrich von Munchhausen (1720–1797), a German army officer whose boasts about his battlefield heroics provided the basis for a humorous best-seller and made his name a byword for preposterous tales.

One common type of Munchhausen consists of people addicted to the surgeon's knife, who will happily swallow foreign objects or injure themselves in order to undergo an operation.

Ellis Fraser, a British fish porter, regularly swallowed large 50p pieces in order to get admitted to the hospital and be looked after by friendly nurses. When caught, he told magistrates that the trick had worked more than seventy times.

Most hospitals keep "black books" listing known bogus patients, like the woman who rushed into the emergency ward with a frighteningly high temperature. It was later discovered that she'd been drawing blood from her arm, mixing it with salad cream, and reinjecting it.

One of the worst cases concerned a six-year-old girl from Yorkshire, England, who was in the hospital twelve times, during which visits she underwent seven major X-ray tests, six examinations under anaesthesia, several unpleasant drug treatments, and had her urine analyzed 150 times. Only after sixteen consultants had given their opinions was it discovered that the girl was perfectly healthy. Her mother had been tampering with the urine samples and falsifying her symptoms.

BONES

Bone is a mixture of organic and mineral matter: a fibrous protein called collagen and tiny crystals of calcium phosphate, which form a mineral known as apatite.

If you remove the apatite by dipping a bone in acid, it becomes so rubbery that you can tie it in a knot. On the other hand, if the collagen is destroyed, the bone becomes extremely brittle. The minerals give bone its hardness but the collagen gives it strength.

Bones in the penis occur in many mammal species such as whales, dolphins, walruses, seals, dogs, cats, rats, mice, monkeys, and apes. Among the primates and carnivores, only humans and hyenas don't have a penis bone. The same is true of clitoris bones in the females of the species.

The mammoth-hunters who inhabited central Europe and Asia some twenty thousand years ago built their dwellings out of the bones of their prey. Massive limb and jaw bones formed the foundation, while ribs and tusks made up the walls and the roof. One site excavated in Russia revealed a hut sixteen feet in diameter built with four hundred separate bones from thirty-three mammoths.

The disease known as "lion head," or *leontiasis*, involves the proliferation of the bones of the face, which gradually cause the holes in the skull occupied by eyes, nostrils, and mouth to close up, producing a truly grotesque appearance. In extreme cases, the eyeballs are squeezed until they bulge right out.

BOOTS

Power-assisted boots were first developed by researchers at the Ufimsky Aviation Institute in Soviet Asia in 1976. The boots are fitted with miniature gasoline-powered internal combustion engines that are attached to each side of the uppers, enabling the wearer to take nine-foot-long strides and travel at sixteen miles an hour. Gas consumption is low, but long-distance, power-assisted walkers are advised to carry a spare can of fuel.

BORES

Leicester University once held a Golden Pillow Award contest for the most boring lecturer of the year. The winner was physicist Dr. Ashley Clarke, who spoke on the classical mechanical formalism for motion in an infinite viscous medium.

Runner-up for the Silver Pillow, which was stuffed with shredded papers on boring lectures, was Dr. Douglas Cossar, who talked on the German vocabulary, particularly words for parts of the leg below the ankle.

BRAHE'S CASTLE

On the morning of August 8, 1576, when the sun was rising together with Jupiter in the heart of Leo, and while the moon was in the western heavens of Aquarius, Danish astronomer Tycho Brahe (1546–1601) laid the foundation stone of Uranieborg, his fairy-tale castle on Hvem Island. On top of the twenty-two-foot-high outer walls in the north and south corners, he built minor replicas of the castle to house his servants and printing press. Two English watchdogs in suitably designed kennels crowned the east and west gates, positioned so that "their barks might announce the arrival of people from any direction." The astronomer continued to manufacture astronomical instruments too large to fit either of the castle's two twenty-two-foot-diameter observatory towers and he eventually left the island in 1597. Today, very little remains of the castle.

BRAIN

The oldest preserved brain matter yet unearthed is six thousand years old and was discovered by archaeologists at Sarasota, Florida. Also in the dig were an extinct tortoise skewered by a stake, and a ten-thousand-year-old boomerang.

A retired English film studio manager, John Clogg, is a man in a thousand million with a very rare brain condition known as "double hemisphere action." As a result, he can simultaneously write different sentences with his right and left hands *and* carry on a quite unconnected conversation. Leonardo da Vinci is believed to have had the same ability, but Clogg says of his talent, "It's never been a bit of use."

Brains are getting heavier. Examination of post-mortem records shows that the average male brain weight has increased from 1,372 grams in 1860 to 1,424 grams today. Women's brains have also put on weight, from 1,242 to 1,265 grams, and in recent years have been growing almost as fast as men's.

W. Grey Walter, one of the great British cyberneticians, believed that everyone has a unique "brainprint" made up of the electrical activity in the brain. He once described our knowledge of what a brainprint was as follows: "We are rather in the position of a visitor from Mars who is deaf and dumb and has no conception of the nature of sound, but is trying to build up a knowledge of languages by looking at the grooves in a gramophone record."

The term *brainwashing* was first used by American journalist Edward Hunter during the Korean War as a translation of the Chinese colloquialism *hsi nao* (wash brain).

The first electrical experiments on the brain were carried out by two medical officers of the Prussian army after the Battle of Sedan in 1870. Officers Fritsch and Hitzig wandered through the battlefield testing their galvanic current on exposed brains and found that, when stimulated by the current, certain areas at the side of the brain produced movements in the opposite side of the body.

Internal brain signals are powered by electrical currents of 50 to 150 microvolts. An electrode on the scalp will record about a tenth of this current in the form of brain waves, which has led scientists to hypothesize that sixty thousand scalps together might supply enough voltage to power a flashlight bulb.

In an experiment conducted by Dr. Adrian Upton at McMaster University in Hamilton, Ontario, an electroencephalogram was connected to a mold of lime jello—and it exhibited signals which, if emitted by a human brain, would indicate life. Dr. Upton says he was probably picking up stray electrical signals, and claims to have made a point about the accuracy of the EEG in determining human brain death.

BREASTS

In Victorian times the marketing of methods for improving the breasts was a growth industry with a variety of different prescriptions.

For reducing the size of the breasts it was recommended that ten grams of iron, ten grams of alum, sixty grams of vinegar, and one hundred grams of water should be mixed with breadcrumbs into a creamy paste to be spread on the breasts and left overnight.

Flabby breasts were treated with white wax and alcohol. To enlarge breasts it was recommended to eat black grapes, drink a special kind of tea, and rub the bosom with a mixture composed of tincture of myrrh, pimpernel and elderflower water, musk, and spirits of wine. Another supposedly foolproof method was to bathe in twenty pounds of fresh strawberries.

In order to investigate the changes that occur in breasts over a monthly cycle, scientists at the Medical Research Council's Unit of Reproductive Biology in Britain enlisted the help of four girl students who, three times a day for three months, knelt on the floor and immersed their breasts in a seven-inch mixing bowl full of water. By measuring the amount of water spilled, scientists were then able to work out the volume of the girls' vital statistics.

BURIALS

Dr. William Price, a Victorian supporter of cremation, ordered in his will that his body be burned on a hilltop in front of invited spectators. Threepence a head was charged, and twenty thousand people showed up to watch.

The owner of a cemetery in Livingston, Montana, was sentenced to dig graves by hand after he was convicted of hiding bodies instead of burying them. Police found thirty unburied corpses in a mausoleum.

Alfred Schmitz of Oregon has patented a method of vertical burial to save space. In order to stop the corpse from slumping to the bottom of the coffin, it is fitted with molded plastic wedges that hold the body upright under the armpits and crotch. The coffin also contains a spring-loaded valve to prevent the buildup of pressure from fluids and gases inside.

There is also a Society for Perpendicular Interment in Melbourne, Australia, which believes that people should be buried upright in cylindrical cardboard coffins.

In 1978, the *Brazil Herald* reported: "Municipal authorities in Sao Joao de Meriti, State of Rio, where a new cemetery is being built, felt it necessary the other day to stress that the cemetery has not been officially opened yet, and would murderers therefore refrain from dumping dead bodies of victims on the site, as has frequently happened lately."

CAMERAS AND
    CAMERAMEN
CANNIBALISM
CARS AND THEIR
    OWNERS
CATTLE
CENSORSHIP
CHE AND CASTRO
CHEMICALS
CHILD CRIME
CHINESE

CIRCUSES AND
    CARNIVALS
CITIES
CLOTHES
CLUBS AND
    SOCIETIES
COCAINE
COMPUTERS
CRAZES
CROCODILES
CURSES

CAMERAS AND CAMERAMEN

Swedish film cameraman Leonard Henriksson, on assignment in Chile, filmed his own killers as he was shot at close range.

On the fourth Sunday of Advent, 1941, at Ozarovo on the Russian front, a German lance corporal named Teitz spotted an immobile group of Russian troops and their horses. They had been ordered to halt for a rest and had frozen to death, preserved as they stood like a monument. As he tried to photograph the scene, Teitz's tears froze over the viewfinder and the shutter seized up.

Louis Daguerre took the first known photograph of a living person in 1839, on a Paris boulevard. Due to an exposure time of several minutes, moving objects made no impression on the silvered plate. The only visible person is a Parisian who, unaware of the camera, paused for a shoeshine.

The largest instant camera in the world is a Polaroid machine at the Museum of Fine Arts in Boston, where it is used to make immaculate copies of famous paintings. Measuring sixteen by twelve by sixteen feet, its interior is equipped with a table, a telephone, and a wastebasket, and can accommodate ten people who wear snooperscopes so that they can see in the dark. The giant film, up to eight feet wide, is pulled down through rollers, spread on the floor, and left for thirty seconds until it is ready to be peeled apart. Because no enlargement is required, the photographs are so good that each brushstroke in a painting can be distinguished.

CANNIBALISM

When Tokyo gang leader Shoichi Murakamie was knifed to death in 1978, his body was cut into little pieces to avoid identification. To get rid of fingerprints, his hands were put in a large pot of soup being cooked at a Chinese street stall and were eaten by at least fifty unsuspecting people.

"Cannibal Khalilullah" ate parts of human bodies in a medical college for three years before his arrest in Dacca on April 3, 1975. Police dragged him away while he was devouring the heart of a dissected corpse. He later admitted: "I get the urge every two weeks or so and then nothing can stop me."

To termites, cannibalism is a way of life and they practice it far more intensely than any other social insect group. In one species the royal couple first build and then seal their nuptial cell, whereupon they eat one to five of the terminal segments of each other's antennae. Three days later they copulate for the first time and later, when rearing their first brood, they eat some of the eggs and young larvae, as well as eggshells and other debris. Cannibalism in termites is usually explained as a protein deficiency.

CARS AND THEIR OWNERS

The longest automobile in the world, an $80,000 custom-built Cadillac, belongs to Leo Weiser, a New York driving-school owner. It is copper colored, and its interior, decorated in Italian velvet, has two sofas, closed-circuit TV, a stereo system, two refrigerators, a bar, and three telephones. The car is twenty-six feet, nine inches long.

Bhatia Karani, a Dubai businessman, has a gold-plated Rolls-Royce Phantom IV Landaulette which comes complete with dual air conditioners, TV, a cocktail bar, an intercom system, and a special alarm which rings if anyone tries to steal the famous "flying lady" from the hood. It cost Mr. Karani $146,125, with the gold-plating alone costing $6,800. A similar car was built for Queen Elizabeth II on her Jubilee; hers cost $34,000 less.

In 1929, Paramount Pictures had a limousine built to look like a steam locomotive. Used to take film stars to the big premieres, it is now owned by a car collector in Florida.

John Dodd, a British mechanic, built himself a car called The Beast, which had a Rolls-Royce Merlin airplane engine, an American-style body, and parts from a tank. He drove it from Stuttgart to Ostend, more than 320 miles, in just three hours and ten minutes. The Beast could tow a one-ton trailer at 107.5 miles an hour. Dodd claimed it had the best power-to-weight ratio of any car in the world, but sadly The Beast burst into flames and had to be destroyed.

A double car was built for a Mid-Island auto dealership in Long Island, New York. The car has two transmissions, two motors, and two dashboards. It took nine months to build, is twenty-one feet long, weighs five tons, and cost $120,000.

CATTLE

Identity cards have been issued for all of Israel's 300,000 cattle.

The Moscow Circus has a troupe of dancing cows that sway to the sound of Russian music and play football.

A calf was born in Israel in early 1978 which had three mouths, three jaws, three sets of gums, and two tongues. It was able to feed through all three mouths.

The beefalo, a cross between a buffalo and a domestic beef breed, was perfected in 1973 by Mr. D. C. Basolo, a rancher from Tracy, California. He had been cross-breeding for fifteen years, producing only sterile offspring, before he was successful.

Mr. Basolo claims that beefalo meat is higher in protein and lower in fat than beef, and that the animal matures quicker than cattle and eats cheaper food. In October, 1975, he told the European media that the beefalo is "the most dramatic breakthrough in the international beef industry in the twentieth century."

CENSORSHIP

In Russia in 1851, during the reign of Nicholas I, censorship reached such extremes that Count S. Urarov, the former Minister of Public Instruction, was not allowed to use the word *demos* in his book on Greek antiquities, nor could he say that Roman emperors were killed, only that they'd "perished." The censor, Akhmator, banned the expression "forces of nature" in a scientific work, and stopped a book on arithmetic because between the figures of a problem he saw a row of dots. A commission was established to examine all music in case it contained conspiratorial messages in code.

CHE AND CASTRO

According to Gardner Miller, a member of the U.S. Army Special Forces unit that trapped and killed Che Guevara in Bolivia in October, 1967, the CIA tracked the revolutionary with infrared devices mounted in U-2 spy planes.

"Guevara had a severe asthmatic condition," Miller said. "The jungle was extremely humid, and he carried a small wood stove to relieve his condition, which registered on the U-2's infrared film, and it was a simple matter to follow him. There was no question who it was—who else would use a stove in hundred-degree temperatures?"

Fidel Castro used to be a film extra in Hollywood before becoming politically involved. He appeared in such films as *Bathing Beauties*, with Esther Williams.

According to band leader Xavier Cugat: "He was a young, ambitious, attractive boy . . . and he had aspirations for being discovered. He was a typical Latin looker, so he was in quite a lot of crowd scenes in those big, splashy films set against a Latin background."

Cugat also claims he was a "complete ham."

CHEMICALS

The number of identified chemicals now stands at four million substances and is growing at the rate of about six thousand a week. A list kept on a computer by the American Chemical Society shows that ninety-six percent of them are organic substances isolated from natural materials or synthesized in laboratories.

CHILD CRIME

A thirteen-year-old boy robbed the Miami police of three pistols, hundreds of bullets, a badge, a hand computer, five electronic bleepers, handcuffs, several cylinders of Mace, and a nightstick.

In Liège, Belgium, a gang of seven boys, aged eight to fifteen, were arrested for stealing thousands of francs worth of toys and clothes. The ringleader, aged eight, was caught after he took to parading around town in a 27,000-franc coat, carrying two guns.

Two ten-year-old boys held up a bank in Buffalo, New York, but ran away when the manager stood up from his desk. The man later told police that he had forgotten his glasses and thought they were midget gunmen.

CHINESE

Chinese is the mother tongue of almost one-third of the world's population, but because its alphabet consists of a minimum of 4,500 characters (ideograms), it is extremely unsuited to modern communications. Chinese compositors still have to select their type by hand from enormous racks. Using a Chinese typewriter has been described as "a cumbersome form of miniature dive-bombing" at which the expert is lucky to achieve a speed of ten words a minute.

CIRCUSES AND CARNIVALS

In 1966, the average age of a circus performer was forty-three; in 1978, it was twenty-three.

The Greatest Show On Earth, the billing Phineas Taylor Barnum gave to his circus, is a copyrighted name. The circus is now a wholly-owned subsidiary of the Mattel Toy Corporation.

When John Ringling North took over The Greatest Show On Earth, one of his greatest stunts was to get Stravinsky to write the music for the elephant's ballet and to hire George Balanchine to choreograph it.
The North circus was run by five brothers from Baraboo, Wisconsin, who started their menagerie with a single hyena.

Among the jobs in the circus itemized in *Logistics of the American Circus*, by Joe McKennon, are such duties as banner tacker, bug man, inside lecturer, connection ticket seller, donniker man, skinner, bull hand, and dog boy.

Every clown has a totally unique "face," which has to be registered after being painted on an eggshell. When a clown dies, his "face" is buried with him.

The first human cannonball was a woman, Zazel. She was fired from a cannon powered by elastic springs on April 2, 1877, at London's Westminster Aquarium. She was shot sixty feet and her act caused such a sensation that her original engagement was extended for two years at a salary of £120 per week. She lived to a ripe old age and died of natural causes in 1937.

Karl Wallenda, one of the foremost wire-walkers in the history of the circus, was the son of a catcher in a flying act. He performed on the wire for fifty-seven years, drawing virtually his entire family into the act and ruling them with an iron hand.

The Great Wallendas had many narrow escapes. They were on the wire when the Hartford fire broke out in the Ringling Brothers circus tent in 1944; 168 people died, but the Wallendas escaped with merely singed costumes. They were also on the wire when the Managuan earthquake struck—but escaped unharmed.

To make the act more spectacular, the Wallendas performed without a safety net. Their supreme stunt was the seven-person pyramid, which no act had attempted before or has duplicated since. It fell apart in Detroit, on the night of January 30, 1962; two men died, another was paralyzed from the waist down, and Karl fractured his pelvis.

From then on, tragedy dogged the Wallendas, culminating in Karl's own death fall at the age of seventy-three. At his widow's request, the balancing pole he had been carrying on that fatal day in Puerto Rico was returned to Sarasota, Florida. It was cut into small pieces and auctioned off to raise funds for the Showfolks of Sarasota.

In the language of the carnival showmen: a *forty-miler* is a carnival which plays close to home; a *rag* is a small animal toy or doll; a *slum* is junk stock—whistles, hoops, ballpoint pens.

CITIES

Moscow was founded in 1147 A.D., by Prince Yuri Dolguruki, whose name means "long arm." His mother was *English*.

The Kremlin wall was designed by three *Italian* architects. Part of it contains the ashes of several *Americans* including John Reed, author of *Ten Days That Shook the World*; Bill Haywood, the IWW leader; Charles Ruthenberg, one-time head of the American Communist Party; and the writer Paxton Hibben.

The Russian name for the city, Moskva, is *Finnish* in origin.

Venice, Rome, Moscow, Cairo, Warsaw, Dublin, Berlin, Toronto, Amsterdam, and Vienna are all names of towns in Ohio.

After heavy Allied bombing at the end of World War II, West Berliners rebuilt their city with salvageable rubble from the ruins—some 230,000 tons of metal and nine million cubic yards of brick. There was enough rubble to construct twenty Great Pyramids. The total street surface rebuilt or repaired would pave a highway thirty-five feet wide from West Berlin to North Africa.

CLOTHES

The mackintosh is so called (though wrongly spelled) after its inventor, Charles Macintosh, a Scotsman who was one of the pioneers of the chemical industry. Charles was born in 1766, and was brought up at his father's fortress-like dye-making works. The factory and the workers' houses were surrounded by a ten-foot wall; the workers were all Gaelic-speaking Highlanders who lived under military discipline, with a roll call every night. Thus were early industrial secrets protected. Charles patented his waterproof fabric in 1823, and advertised the coats as "life preservers" for stagecoach drivers, horsemen, mariners, and others who had to face the rigors of the weather.

Moss Bros., the London-based clothing-for-hire firm, supplied fifty thousand Allied officers with uniforms during World War II. They were once contracted by a Danish department store to supply fifty bowler hats, which were then used for geranium pots in a window display.

The Lazarone Chevron bulletproof vest is made of plastic, weighs only three and a half pounds, and can stop a .38-caliber bullet at point-blank range.

An American firm, Tee-Hee T-Shirts of New York City, sells scented T-shirts which release twenty-four smells, including orange, pine, banana, and beer, through the action of the wearer's body heat.

President Nixon's tastelessness was shown in the special uniforms he ordered for the White House guards. Only worn at state dinners during his presidency, the uniforms consisted of white tunics, black gunbelts, visored caps, and yards of gold braid—more appropriate to Ruritania than Washington, D.C. Since Nixon's demise, the uniforms have been gathering dust in a government warehouse—embarrassing souvenirs which the Secret Service cannot burn because destruction of Federal property is a crime.

A design-a-uniform competition for the French army, with a first prize of 150,000 francs, led to the following suggestions:

Andres Courrèges sketched a black soldier fitted out in sky blue with tricolor braces and calf-high jungle boots, with yellow socks and a baseball cap.

Louis Feraud preferred uniforms decorated with embroidered flowers, gold buttons, and real blooms covering the helmet. Feraud admitted: "I also like bow ties," and commented, "the army would be much more gay."

Michel Renoma favored polo neck pullovers, felt jackets with plenty of shoulder padding, tartan scarves, and brown leather laced cavalry boots.

The scarlet tunics of the Vatican Swiss Guard are the oldest uniforms in the world. Originally designed by Michelangelo, they remained unchanged for 450 years—until 1975, that is, when they were modified for the first time, so that guards could carry tear gas grenades.

CLUBS AND SOCIETIES

The American Tentative Society is a group dedicated to the view that all knowledge is tentative. After ten years it has four officers, no members, and no fixed policy.

In his book *Anatomy of Britain*, Anthony Sampson retells one of the legends of the Beefsteak Club, which is located opposite a striptease joint in Leicester Square, and where all the waiters are called Charles.

The story goes that in the period before World War I, the police got suspicious when they saw elderly gentlemen emerging in good spirits from the club every night and, assuming it was a brothel, raided it.

They found four men sitting at a long table, and a policeman asked who they were. One of them said he was the Lord Chancellor, another the Archbishop of Canterbury, and a third the Governor of the Bank of England.

The policeman turned to the fourth man and said, "I suppose that you're the Prime Minister."

"As a matter of fact I am," said Arthur Balfour, the Prime Minister.

London's Garrick Club, founded in 1831, is only kept in the black by its share of the royalties of *Winnie the Pooh*, bequeathed by author A. A. Milne.

The German Society for the Promotion of Noncommercial Donaldism was founded in Hamburg in May, 1977, by thirty enthusiasts of Donald Duck. They have a song, a constitution, a newsletter, and aim to establish a Donald Duck chair at the local university. Club president Hans von Storch, a twenty-seven-year-old meteorologist, says: "We have banded together to study the history and meaning of this world-famous, all-too-human cartoon character. But we are doing it with humor. Anything else would be insane."

One of the most exclusive clubs ever was the Jekyll Club, whose members included such Robber Barons of the 1890s as J. Pierpont Morgan, Henry Clay Frick (founder of the U.S. Steel Corporation), Joseph Pulitzer, E. H. Goodyear, and J. D. Rockefeller and Walter Jennings of Standard Oil. The club was situated on Jekyll Island off the coast of Georgia, and became a retreat for the billionaires in the winter months. At one time it was said that its members controlled one-sixth of the U.S.A.'s wealth. Its excellent hunting facilities were improved by a gift of three hundred wild boar from King Umberto of Italy. The island was bought by the state of Georgia in 1947, for $650,000.

Overeaters Victorious, Inc. is a group from Minneapolis that believes in "dieting with Jesus." Among the titles that are suggested reading for the group are: *God's Answer to Fat* by Frances Hunter and *More of Jesus, Less of Me* by Joan Cavanaugh.

Ms. Cavanaugh recommends that Christian dieters should: "Only buy foods that Jesus, or John or Peter would buy." She continues: "God gives us the good stuff. I can't imagine Jesus Christ coming out of the supermarket with twelve bags of potato chips, one for each apostle."

Alan Abel, a professional comedian since the late 1950s, once launched a hoax Society for Indecency to Naked Animals, whose aim was to promote the wearing of underwear by cows, pigs, and other animals to preserve their modesty.

Before the Trekkies came the International Wizard of Oz Club, founded in January, 1957, by a fourteen-year-old schoolboy, Justin Schiller, now a rare-book dealer in New York. It has two thousand members including Warren Hollister, proud owner of the pencil with which L. Frank Baum wrote *The Wonderful Wizard of Oz*. It is insured for $40,000. Every year the Munchkins meet in the East, the Gillikins in the North, and the Winkies in the West.

COCAINE

Sigmund Freud bought his first sample of cocaine from the drug company Merck—on credit. It cost $1.27 a gram.

In the 1880s, the Toronto Lacrosse Club of Canada, who won the title "Champion of the World," trained on cocaine.

Given a choice between pressing a button that dispenses food and another that dispenses cocaine, laboratory monkeys consistently preferred the drug, and consumed it "almost exclusively for up to eight days," according to a study by Drs. Thomas Aigner and Robert Balster of Virginia Commonwealth University.

COMPUTERS

Computers are supposed to be unemotional machines, but Humphrey, the GEC 2050 computer that runs the accounts and the box office at London's Wembley Conference Centre, has clear misogynist tendencies. It is quite happy to be programmed by a man, but every time a woman tries to communicate with it, Humphrey displays the sign "Illegal Entry."

A computer dating service for dogs, named Selectadog, is run by Pedigree Petfoods. The potential owner fills in a seventeen-question form and is matched with a dog from a range of fifty-seven popular breeds. In the first two years of operation, many people complained they had been matched with the one breed of dog they hated.

Of the 200,000 computers at work in the U.S., only two hundred are rated "secure" by computer experts. All of these are machines used by the FBI, the Pentagon, the CIA, the National Security Agency, and the State Department.

Computers can be reprogrammed by crooked operators and used to embezzle and defraud. Computer espionage is another problem. In 1976, the Secret Service rewired its computer circuits so only a handful of coded agents could gain access to its memory containing a list of forty thousand potential political assassins.

A disgruntled employee of a West Coast firm wrote out a computer program so that six months after he had left, the computer would erase every account in its memory. This worked so successfully that the company had no record of who owed them how much money, so they could not send out any bills. In desperation, they advertised for people to pay up, and when no one did, they went bankrupt.

CRAZES

The yo-yo was first introduced commercially to the West by Donald Duncan, who noticed Filipino sailors playing with stones on strings by the San Francisco wharf. They were originally used for stoning enemies, allowing the stone to be retrieved afterward.

Yo-yos were first introduced into Britain in 1820.

One claim for the origin of the Hula-Hoop is that it began with children in the Sydney backstreets who would remove the loops from old casks and spin them with their bodies.

In the 1950s, Hula-Hoops became a $20 million industry. They were sold, among other things, as slimming aids, but ended up causing an increase in back complaints. Hula-Hoops were banned in Japan because they caused so many traffic accidents.

Pogo sticks became a craze among the upper crust of Paris in the 1920s after an explorer brought back a sketch of a stick used by the Dyaks in Borneo for sacrificial dances. The pogo stick craze boomed again in the 1960s.

CROCODILES

The old myth that crocodiles eat their young is not as far astray as one might think. After the young crocs hatch, their mother gently takes them into her huge jaws and shakes them down into a special pouch in the floor of her mouth. Then, with up to eighteen baby crocodiles peering out from between her teeth, she takes them down to the water for their introduction to the aquatic life.

CURSES

In ancient Greece, curses were often scratched on pieces of pottery or lead tablets and buried in the ground—with the result that a number have been preserved. One from 400 B.C. says simply, "I put quartan fever on Aristion to the death."

An Athenian example from the fourth century A.D. was aimed at disabling the man's opponents in a court case: "I bind Theagenes in tongue and soul, and the speech that he is preparing. I bind also the hands and feet of Pyrrhias the cook, his tongue and his soul and the speech that he is preparing."

After similarly binding two further witnesses, the curse ends: "All this I bind, obliterate, bury, impale."

The world's leading expert on curses is Reinhold Aman, founder of the International Research Center for Verbal Aggression, which publishes a scholarly journal, *Maledicta*.

Among the curses he has collected in his researches are a three-thousand-year-old Egyptian hieroglyphic curse, a modern Ghanaian curse which describes a man's sexual organ as being "as bent as the gearshift of a Mercedes Benz," and the Esperanto curse "fiulaco" which means "disgusting person."

DANGEROUS DRIVING

DEATH

DECAPITATION FEATS

DEMOLITION

DIAMONDS

DILDOS

DIRECTORS AND PRODUCERS

DISASTER STAGER

DIVINATION

DIVORCE

DOGS

DOLLS

DOODLES

DREAMS

DANGEROUS DRIVING

In 1972, a California motorist admitted to dangerous driving, but pleaded that his attention was distracted by the shrieks of a woman passenger who was being nipped by a lobster.

DEATHS

Do people subconsciously control when they die? Dr. Philip Kunz, a Utah sociologist, studied the relationship between death and birthdays and found that nearly half the people in his sample had died within three months of their birthday. That's twice the expected rate.

After a wedding in Bloemfontein, South Africa, the bridegroom's mother was knocked down and killed by the happy couple's limousine.

A Hungarian hunter, Endre Bascany, was so good at imitating the love call of a stag that another hunter shot him.

One of the fastest runners ever was Griffith Morgan, a Welshman born in 1696, who trained with his local hunt and often outran the hounds. At the age of thirty-seven, so the story goes, he ran twelve miles in fifty-three minutes to win a purse of one hundred sovereigns. Unfortunately, after the race, a well-wisher slapped Morgan on the back and he fell down dead.

Deadly coincidence? Two brothers in Bermuda were killed while riding the same moped in the same street by the same taxi and driver, carrying the same passenger—but a year apart.

A twenty-nine-year-old American student, Robert Antosczyk, became the first recorded case of death by yoga.

He fell into a deep trance and, two days later, was discovered dead—still in the same classical yoga position. Scientists believe the trance slowed down his heart until it stopped.

Choking is now the sixth most common form of accidental death in the United States, according to the National Safety Council. Steak, lobster tails, hard-boiled eggs, and bread get fatally stuck in some 2,500 throats every year. Choking is more lethal than lightning, snakebites, air crashes, and even gun mishaps.

Loneliness is a killer—literally. A study by Dr. James Lynch of the University of Maryland found that unmarried people—whether single, divorced, or widowed—are between two and five times more likely to die of heart disease than married people. They are also more likely to die of cirrhosis of the liver and lung cancer, or to be killed in a car crash.

DECAPITATION FEATS

One of the oldest magic tricks known to man is the decapitation feat. We know that it was performed by a magician for the Pharaoh Cheops, builder of the Great Pyramid, three thousand years before Christ, because it's fully described in hieroglyphics.

The trick was also part of the repertoire of American Indian magicians before the white man came.

One of the most spectacular decapitation feats ever staged was performed by American illusionist Will Rock during the 1930s and '40s. Against the background of a French Revolution scene, he was locked into a giant guillotine, and when the blade fell, his head was actually seen to drop into the basket. This same illusion was used by rock star Alice Cooper, staged by The Amazing Randi.

How does it work? That's still the magicians' trade secret.

DEMOLITION

In 1975, a team of forty karate experts demolished twelve terraced houses at Poolsbrook, near Chesterfield in England, using only their heads, hands, and feet. It was a charity stunt.

DIAMONDS

Diamonds are a thief's as well as a girl's best friend. The four C's of the diamond business—cut, clarity, carat and color—do not give an accurate identification of individual diamonds. Things got so bad that police often found themselves returning stolen diamonds to known thieves because they had no means of identifying them as stolen goods. This problem has now been solved by Israeli physicist Shmuel Shtrikman, who discovered that if you shine a beam of laser light into the "table" or top facet of a diamond, it will send back its own unique pattern of reflections, as distinctive as a fingerprint.

DILDOS

Dildos, or artificial penises, are one of the oldest forms of sex aids. The Greek writer Heronda in the third century B.C. says that dildos were made of leather by the local cobbler and were so expensive that several women had to share one among them. The Romans mainly used them for deflowering virgins.

DIRECTORS AND PRODUCERS

William Castle, the film director who established a reputation as the "king of gimmicks," once offered free life insurance to all viewers of his movie *Macabre* in case they died of fright. The total insurance was provided by Lloyd's of London at a cost of $5,000. A special preview of the film was arranged in an abandoned cemetery, the movie being screened on a tomb.

For his movie *Homicidal,* audiences were offered a refund if they left during the "fright break" ten minutes before the end. No wonder Castle's autobiography was called *Step Right Up! I'm Gonna Scare the Pants Off America.*

Walt Disney was the only Hollywood film producer to be honored with a commemorative postage stamp. It was issued in the United States in 1968.

Robert L. Lippert, a Hollywood producer for nearly twenty-five years, once shot five Westerns concurrently, using the same cast, locations, and sets. Lippert saved money by filming all the chases, barroom scenes, and brawls simultaneously, and brought all the movies home for $50,000 each.

DISASTER STAGER

W. Bruce Smith earned his living by staging disasters in dramatic plays. Among his most famous scenes were floods, shipwrecks, and the chariot race in the stage version of *Ben-Hur.*

He once staged a "sandstorm" using ground-up cork. It worked until someone opened a door backstage and the "sand" was blown over the first eight rows in the Drury Lane Theatre, London.

He died at the age of ninety—during a fit of laughter.

DIVINATION

The following are the technical terms for some of the methods of divination, or predicting the future:

Aeromancy	—by atmospheric phenomena
Alectromancy	—by a cock picking up grain
Arithmancy	—by numbers
Austromancy	—by the winds
Bibliomancy	—by random passages in a book

Beltonism	—by water currents
Capnomancy	—by smoke
Catoptromancy	—by mirrors
Ceromancy	—by molten wax dropped in water
Cledomancy	—from chance events or statements
Crystallomancy	—by looking in crystal balls
Dowsing	—by a divining rod or pendulum
Geoloscopy	—by a person's manner of laughing
Gyromancy	—by whirling around until dizziness causes a fall
Halomancy	—by grains of salt
Haruspicy	—from the entrails of animals
Hydromancy	—by water
Ichthyomancy	—by fishes
Lampadomancy	—by the flame of a candle or torch
Leconomancy	—by the shape of oil poured on water
Margaritomancy	—by pearls
Moleosophy	—by moles on the body
Myomancy	—by the movements of mice
Oneiromancy	—by dreams
Onychomancy	—by the fingernails
Ophiomancy	—by the movements of snakes
Pegomancy	—by fountains
Pessomancy	—by pebbles
Pyromancy	—by looking into the fire
Scapulomancy	—by the shoulder blades of animals
Scatoscopy	—by the examination of excrement
Spideromancy	—by the movements of straws on a red-hot iron
Spodomancy	—from ashes
Tephromancy	—from sacrificial ashes
Uromancy	—by urine
Xylomancy	—by dry sticks
Zoomancy	—by the behavior of animals

DIVORCE

Traditional or folk divorce occurred in England as recently as the nineteenth century. If a man was fed up with his wife, he could get rid of her simply by putting her on public sale for not less than one shilling. The man who bought her automatically became her husband. On April 7, 1832, a farmer named Joseph Thompson sold his wife of three years at Carlisle, in northern England, for twenty shillings and a Newfoundland dog.

DOGS

Pekingese are very rare in Peking.

A sheepdog trial in California was won by a dog called Arch—who had only three legs.

In April, 1976, the newspaper *Leninskoya Znamya* reported that the Soviet Union's first grooming salon for dogs had opened in Moscow. The manager was quoted as saying: "Here qualified craftsmen can do any hairstyle for your four-legged friend."

A San Francisco dentist, Dr. Ursula Dietrich, has invented a toothpaste for dogs called Doggydent, which tastes of beef and sells for five dollars a tube.

Dr. Daniel Tortora, an animal psychologist and author of *Help! This Animal Is Driving Me Crazy*, believes that, just like humans, dogs can develop phobias. He claims they can also have complexes about such things as thunderstorms, televisions, refrigerators, telephone bells, and even music.

Kathy Coon, a Baton Rouge psychologist, has developed an IQ test manual for dogs.

Stan, the first dog in Spain to wear contact lenses, was knocked down by a car and killed the day after the fitting while crossing a road near Bilbao.

Dogs who travel frequently on the buses and trams of the Hague, the Dutch capital, can hold a young person's season ticket. All they need is an identity card with their photo, name, and owner's name.

Sound-activated dog collars, which give their animals an electric shock when they bark, are for sale under such brand names as Wuf-E-Nuf and No Bark Collar. They sometimes give shocks strong enough to burn a dog's neck, and can be triggered by inappropriate noises such as hand-clapping, cars hooting, or another dog barking.

In July, 1978, an elderly woman in Johannesburg, South Africa, was seriously injured when she was struck on the head by a falling dog. The animal, a miniature Pomeranian, had been thrown from the top of a thirteen-story building by vandals.

The world's longest dogsled race covers one thousand miles of rugged Alaskan terrain. The 1978 winner crossed the finish line after fourteen days, eighteen hours, fifty-two minutes, and twenty-four seconds.

Benji, the film-star dog who won the Patsy (Picture Animal Top Star of the Year Award) in 1977, is so popular in Bangkok that a picture of his head, five stories high, is on permanent public display. His handler reports that when he takes Benji on trips, people stop bellhops and ask for the dog's room number.

Caliph, a Great Dane, won a place in British legal history when he bit the hand of a judge while on trial for his life— for biting.

The first Lassie was, in fact, a red-haired male dog who sired a son that took his place in the TV series. The various Lassies won eight Patsys in eight years, an unbroken record, and earned $60,000 in 1967 alone.

So many American dog-lovers asked for the paw print of Gerald Ford's retriever, Patsy, that a rubber stamp was used to sign the dog's autograph.

In Australia, a black Labrador called Rastus has mastered the art of solo water skiing.

Teddy, a Great Dane who worked for Mack Sennett, could, without any help, fill a kettle, light a stove, make coffee, sweep the floor—all for forty dollars a week.

Rin Tin Tin earned some $44,000 a picture and died in the arms of Jean Harlow in 1932, aged fourteen, after appearing in fifty films. Found abandoned as a puppy in a front-line trench in France during World War I, he was known to the enemies of Warner Brothers as "the mortgage lifter" for his services to that company.

In 1976, the estate of Rin Tin Tin filed suit against filmmaker Michael Winner, claiming that his movie *Won Ton Ton, the Dog That Saved Hollywood*, was based on RTT's life story. Winner commented at the time, "It's absurd to be sued by a dog, especially by a dog who's been dead for the past twenty years."

The movie's premiere was attended by 575 first-nighters, of whom one hundred were dogs. Won Ton Ton, in real life an Alsatian named Gus, arrived in a "limo, sporting a rhinestone collar, and accompanied by his trainer and a social secretary."

DOLLS

Among the more unusual dolls produced by American toy manufacturers is Tuesday Taylor, a bikinied doll that gets a suntan in a minute when you put her under the light. The color lasts for an hour, then fades.

The world's most expensive dollhouse was sold for $256,000 at a Christie's auction in London in 1978. Called "Titania's Palace," it is a masterpiece of craftsmanship containing sixteen rooms, a working chamber organ (which can be played with matchsticks), and a silver clothes press—but no toilet.

DOODLES

During the many conferences that U.S. diplomat Charles Bohlen attended with Joseph Stalin, the Soviet dictator frequently doodled on scrap pads. Later Bohlen recalled that the doodle was always the same—heads of wolves.

DREAMS

Cold-blooded animals such as reptiles and fish do not dream, but warm-blooded ones, including mammals and birds, do. By studying rapid eye movements (REMs) during sleep—which in humans is a sure sign of dreaming—French physiologist Michel Jouvet found that animals invariably dream more when they are younger. Animals like calves and foals, which can fend for themselves immediately after birth, dream more in the womb and less after being born than do animals like kittens and human babies, which are dependent on parental care.

Elias Howe spent years trying to perfect a sewing machine. One night he dreamed that he had been captured by a primitive tribe and was sentenced to be speared to death if he didn't produce a sewing machine within twenty-four hours. Howe racked his brains for the right solution, but in vain. When the deadline was up, the warriors surrounded Howe and raised their spears to kill him. Suddenly Howe woke up, leaped out of bed, and rushed to his laboratory. He had noticed that each spear had an eye-shaped hole near its point and his problem was solved. To make a sewing machine that worked, the hole had to be at the tip of the needle, not at the top or middle.

A social worker in St. Albans, England, was cleared of the charge of maliciously wounding his wife after a jury accepted his strange evidence. He told them he had had a dream of being chased by a mob of football hooligans and lashed out at them in his sleep. When he woke up, he found that he was stabbing his wife with a kitchen knife.

His wife told the court that her husband had shouted, "We are being attacked—I will protect you." She said, "I then tried to wake him by kicking and shouting. I felt another sensation in my chest. When I put the light on, I saw I was covered in blood and there was blood on the bed."

The chemist Kekule developed the important theory of the benzene ring after two occasions when he was half asleep and saw the image "as dancing atoms whirling in a ring, the larger ones forming a chain dragging the smaller ones."

EARTH   ENERGY
EGGS   EUPHEMISMS
EINSTEIN   EVOLUTION
ELEPHANTS   EXPLOSION
THE ELVIS ESTATE   EYES

EARTH

If time were speeded up so that each day contained one million years, each minute would be equivalent to 695 years and each second to 11 years and 7 months. At this pace, the change of the seasons, the annually varying coloration of the globe, the spread and retreat of the polar icefields, would become invisible. Totally new patterns would emerge. The drifting of the continents, building of mountains, erosion of sea shores, eruption and disappearance of volcanic islands, and spreading of deserts would become dominant features. America and Europe would move apart at a steady, majestic pace. India would slowly shrink as it continued to thrust up into the main body of Asia. Ice ages would grow and contract in a period of hours. Men's lives would last about six seconds. Earth would be seen to quiver and shake as its face continuously changed like a living cell.

The rotation of the Earth is gradually slowing down, due to the braking effect of the moon. Fossil records show that some 390 million years ago there were 400 days in a year. The slowing down of the Earth, however, is not continuous; there have been anomalous periods when its rotation has temporarily speeded up. An accelerating Earth is associated with improving climate. For unknown reasons, periods of changeover from acceleration to deceleration, and vice versa, are often accompanied by a dramatic increase in the number of biological species that become extinct. The Earth's rotation has been decelerating for the last 65 million years, but there is now some evidence—disturbances in the magnetic field, gradually worsening weather—that a changeover may be close or even imminent.

The Earth is not an entirely stable planet. It wobbles very slightly, possibly as a result of the disturbance caused by major earthquakes, possibly because of large-scale movements in the atmosphere from one year to the next. The wobble was first accurately observed by a nineteenth-century Boston merchant named Chandler, and is popularly known as the "Chandler wobble," though it is described mathematically as "Eulerian nutation."

EGGS

It takes four hours to hard-boil an ostrich egg. The north African ostrich lays an egg that weighs 31 pounds and can bear the weight of a 250-pound man.

The Goldenlay Egg Cuber is designed for people fed up with the awkward shape of eggs. Recipe: insert one hard-boiled egg, hot from the pan, into the cuber. Add the pressing plate, then gently screw down the lid, thereby applying pressure which deforms the egg—shell and all—into a perfect cube. After cooling for twenty minutes, the cubed egg will retain its unnatural shape indefinitely, which makes for easier stacking or a novelty effect.

A hen in Soviet Estonia is said to have laid an egg containing nine yolks. It weighed 14 ounces, was 5.5 inches high and 2.7 inches wide.

A scientific myth, immortalized in many textbooks, says that it is virtually impossible to boil an egg on a mountain as high as Mont Blanc, because the thin air means water boils at 91 degrees Celsius (196 degrees F.)—at which temperature you'd get frostbite from waiting.

Not so, claim two scientists from the Biochemistry Department at Oxford, who experimented with boiling eggs at reduced pressures and discovered that you can in fact hard-boil an egg at 91 degrees Celsius in just under ten minutes.

English zoologists have developed a fiberglass electronic egg to help them study the habits of breeding birds. Ranging from chicken to swan size and suitably colored, the false eggs are used to replace normal ones in birds' nests. They contain miniature high-frequency radios to transmit data about temperature, humidity, and light as it is received.

Egg City, fifty miles northwest of Los Angeles, is one of the world's largest battery hen units, containing two million birds housed ninety thousand to a building, with five birds in a sixteen-by-eighteen-inch cage. It's run by Julius Goldman, who told a *National Geographic* reporter: "We keep track of the food eaten and the eggs collected in two rows of cages among the 110 rows in the building. When production drops to an uneconomic point, all ninety thousand birds are sold to processors for potpies or chicken soup. It doesn't pay to keep track of every row in the house, let alone individual hens; with two million birds on hand you have to rely on statistical samplings."

EINSTEIN

Albert Einstein gave up his German citizenship in 1894, at age fifteen, because of his hatred of German militarism. He was a stateless person until 1897, when he became a Swiss citizen. In 1910 he also acquired Austro-Hungarian citizenship on taking a university post in Prague. He resumed his German citizenship in 1918, when he was given an appointment in Berlin, but resigned it for the second and last time in 1933. He finally became an American citizen in 1936.

Einstein was a late developer and, even at the age of nine, could not speak fluently. His parents feared that he might be subnormal, and it is probable that in early childhood he suffered from dyslexia, or word-blindness.

Einstein's first major lecture in English was given at an annual meeting of the American Association for the Advancement of Science (AAAS) in the 1930s. The great man was known to be nervous about the speech, and on the morning of the big day a notice appeared in the personals column of the local Pittsburgh paper, inserted by a well-wisher, which read, "Don't be afraid, Albert, I am sure you can do it." Einstein spoke in front of two massive blackboards, which he covered with equations as he spoke. When he remarked that his line of reasoning was quite simple, his audience of high-powered scientists shouted, "No!"

In 1952, Einstein was invited to be President of Israel but he refused, saying, "I know a little about nature but hardly anything about men."

Einstein was absent-minded, even as a student. When he stayed with friends, he frequently forgot his suitcase and often had to knock on his landlady's door in Zurich late at night, calling, "It's Einstein—I've forgotten my key again."

When he heard of the atomic annihilation of Hiroshima in 1945, Einstein said, "Had I known, I would have become a plumber."

Einstein's theory of relativity was officially rejected in China from 1970 to 1978, on the grounds that it was "an example of a reactionary, idealistic, and metaphysical world view." The rejection was later blamed on Mao's widow, Chiang Ching, and the "Gang of Four," who "made ridiculous mistakes regarding the basic concepts of physics."

ELEPHANTS

The elephant is the only animal with four knees.

In Thailand, a white elephant is considered a symbol of good luck. By law, all white elephants found in Thailand must be given to the king. In 1767, the King of Burma was so envious of the Thai king's collection that he invaded the country.

White elephants are not in fact white; their skin is the usual gray. They are albinos, differing only in their pink eyes.

In Los Angeles in 1972, the owner of Bimbo, a circus elephant, was seeking $9,000 damages following a road crash in which, the owner claimed, Bimbo lost her enthusiasm for hopping, skipping, jumping, waltzing, and waterskiing. We have no record whether she got the money.

The first recorded elephant twins were born at Tanzania's Lake Mayara national park in 1976.

In his book *The Last Place On Earth*, Harold T. P. Hayes writes: "Elephants are believed to have some conception of death, and possibly even of the reasons they are hunted. They have been known to seize the tusks from a dead member of the family and smash them to pieces. Here in Uganda, during one of the cropping episodes (a wildlife management euphemism for killing), the ears and feet of the destroyed elephants were stored in a shed to be prepared for sale as handbags and umbrella stands. A group of elephants broke into the shed, removed the objects, and buried them. Scientists involved in the episode are said to feel uncomfortable about the incident."

THE ELVIS ESTATE

The eighty-two-page inventory of Elvis Presley's estate, valued in total at ten million dollars, included a complete inventory of his mansion, Graceland.

The house was filled with statues of tigers, lions, elephants, dogs, birds, a ram, a whale, an eagle, and a dolphin. Elvis collected statuettes of Joan of Arc and Venus de Milo; one of the latter came complete with an electric waterfall.

For transport he had two Stutz Blackhawks, valued at $100,000 each, a Ferrari, a Cadillac, an International Harvester Scout, a Jeep, a Ford Bronco, a custom-built Chevy pickup, three tractors, seven motorcycles, seven golf carts, three mobile homes, and six horses.

He had eighteen TV sets, including two seventeen-inch color sets installed in the ceiling above his nine-foot-square bed. His wardrobe consisted of one hundred pairs of trousers, twenty-one capes, three cartons of shoes, and three jewel-studded vests.

His trophy room was decorated with his army discharge papers, forty-one plaques, thirty-two photo albums of his films, thirty script albums, plus scrapbooks and trophies from fans, record companies, and karate clubs.

His musical instruments included seven guitars, one of which had his name inlaid in mother-of-pearl.

ENERGY

Adults in industrial societies consume about 2.4 kilowatts of energy in all forms, including food, every day, the equivalent of seven gallons of gasoline.

A recent Commerce Department report on the United States' future energy requirements showed that if energy consumption continues to grow at the current rate, the country will need to build a new electric power plant every twelve days between now and the end of the century.

Companies in America and Britain are busily trying to find a cheap, efficient means of turning coal into oil. Not that the idea is new; during World War II, Nazi Germany used a secret process to make coal-derived oil. The method was so successful that by 1945, seventy-five percent of the Reich's fuel needs were provided by synthetic means.

Bruce Hannon of the University of Illinois has calculated that if Americans reduced their meat consumption by only thirty percent, thirty-two million hectares (about eighty million acres) required to feed cattle would be freed for other uses. Only five percent of this area set aside for growing vegetables, including soya beans, would make up the missing protein. The raising of timber, sugarcane, or sunflowers on the remainder would supply enough fuel for 255,000 new one-thousand-megawatt power stations, producing twenty to twenty-five percent of all the country's energy. And all for one meatless day in three.

EUPHEMISMS

The New York Times's "Grand Prize for Euphemism" was awarded to the Central Intelligence Agency for referring to an assassination unit as a "health alteration committee."

The International Whaling Commission describes the time when young whales attain maturity as "reaching the age of recruitment," meaning they can be legally killed.

EVOLUTION

The first known example of the extinction of an animal resulting in the decline of a plant species has been discovered by Dr. Temple, an American wildlife ecologist.

The animal is the dodo, which lived on the Indian Ocean island of Mauritius until it became extinct in 1681. Dodos fed on the *calvaria major* tree, and since the birds died, no new *calvaria* trees have grown. In 1973, there were only thirteen left, none younger than three hundred years.

The theory holds that the bird and the tree evolved together as the tree's fruit stones had such strong shells that they needed to be battered and softened by the dodo's powerful gizzard before they could burst open and germinate.

Dr. Temple tested this theory by feeding the tree's seeds to turkeys and planting the softened stones after they had been digested. Three out of ten seeds germinated, and a new *calvaria* tree began to grow for the first time in three hundred years.

The most famous example of insects adapting to their environment is so-called "industrial melanism." As the industrial revolution spread through the English country-side, producing dark and sooty cities in its wake, the local peppered moths evolved to suit the changing conditions by adopting an increasingly dark brown coloring, which gave them better camouflage on the trunks of urban trees. In recent years, however, since the introduction of clean-air legislation to reduce pollution in Britain, the moths are slowly reverting to their original lighter coloration.

Animals of all kinds tend to grow larger in the course of evolution, a fact enshrined in biology as Cope's Rule. The problem with sheer size is that a given environment can support fewer large animals than small ones, and a population with small numbers is more liable to extinction.

The best known exception to Cope's Rule is the phenomenon of animals that grow smaller when isolated on islands. The limit in geographical mobility somehow counteracts the evolutionary tendency toward growth.

EXPLOSION

A twenty-six-year-old Dane died on the operating table when an electrically heated surgical knife caused his stomach to explode. Dr. Niels Olsen, the surgeon, said the knife had burned through the patient's digestive tract and ignited explosive gases. The explosion was so violent that part of the colon was completely destroyed. In spite of further operations to repair the damage, the patient died of blood poisoning.

EYES

Everyone knows that the size of the pupils changes according to one's interest in a person or object. Less well known is the fact that pupil size increases during any period of active mental attention. Look closely into someone's eyes, then give him or her a seven-digit number to memorize, pause for ten seconds, then ask him or her to repeat the number. You should see the person's pupils expand when you say the number, contract while they memorize it, and expand again when they repeat it.

FERAL CHILDREN
FILMS
FINGERS AND
    FINGERPRINTS
FIRST WORDS
FISH
FLAVORS

FLIGHT
FLOATING ISLAND
FLU
FOOD
FORGERY
FRAUDS
FREAKS

FERAL CHILDREN

Stories of children brought up by animals date back to ancient mythology, and the story of Romulus and Remus. But why wolves should appear so often in these tales has never been explained.

Between 1344 and 1961, some fifty-three feral children have been reported, some of the most recent being a wolf-boy in Lucknow, India; a teenage girl discovered living in the wild with a herd of water buffalo in Sri Lanka; and an ape-boy in the Central African nation of Burundi.

One famous case is that of Amala and Kamala, the wolf-girls of Midnapore. They were discovered in October, 1920, by missionary Reverend Joseph Singh, curled up in a wolf's lair built inside an enormous ant mound. The girls, aged three and five years at the time, could only move around on all fours, were relatively insensitive to heat and cold, slept little, and got on better with dogs than with other children. They howled at night like wolves and their preferred diet was raw meat, particularly animal entrails. The younger girl died within a year of capture, but the elder survived for nine years, gradually learning to walk upright and to speak a few words.

Perhaps the most famous feral child of all was Victor, the wild boy of Aveyron, subject of François Truffaut's film *The Wild Child* (L'Enfant Sauvage). Victor was discovered in a forest in southern France in 1799, when he was eleven years old—naked, speechless, and living like a wild animal. Brought to Paris, he was diagnosed as a congenital idiot and consigned to the care of a doctor called Jean-Marc-Gaspard Itard, who undertook his education.

Although Itard considered his work a failure (he was unable to teach Victor to speak), the doctor went on to become a pioneer in the education of the mentally and physically handicapped and, more than one hundred years later, his teaching methods became the basis of the Montessori system of preschool education.

Victor himself was given a state pension and lived in Paris under the care of his kind but uneducated housekeeper until his death at forty.

FILMS

The Chinese call films "electric shadows."

Universal Studios, built on the site of an old chicken farm, by far the largest set of facilities in the industry, is now California's second biggest tourist attraction, after Disneyland. The studios have thirty-four sound stages, their own mayor, chamber of commerce, post office, and five-hundred-room hotel.

The actors originally cast to star in a movie may never get in the final version:
Lee Marvin was first offered Robert Shaw's part in *Jaws*.
The African Queen was originally to star David Niven and Bette Davis; Niven had previously turned down the role of Hopalong Cassidy in 1935.
Noël Coward was offered James Mason's part in *Lolita*.
Lawrence Olivier was offered the lead in *The Godfather*; the Mafia's preference was for Anthony Quinn.
Lawrence of Arabia was originally planned with Marlon Brando or Albert Finney in mind.
Barbra Streisand hoped to star opposite Elvis Presley in *A Star Is Born*. The rock 'n' roll remake was originally conceived to star Carly Simon and James Taylor.

Extras in Hollywood are now called "atmosphere people."

During the shooting of the fire in *In Old Chicago*, it was considered so dangerous on the set that no women were allowed, and men dressed in long skirts and bonnets doubled for all the women.

The Rank Odeon at Salisbury, Wiltshire, has the only fifteenth-century cinema foyer in the world. When the cinema was built, it was on the site of the ancient house of a local wool merchant, which had a preservation order on it. So now patrons pass through a carefully preserved hall complete with minstrel gallery, carved oak screen, and timbered roof to get to the auditorium.

In 1914, D. W. Griffith was so short of cash that he filmed *Battle of the Sexes* in just four days, to enable him to pay his stars, Owen Moore and Lillian Gish.

Lawsuits between disgruntled movie stars over their billing are not uncommon. Actor Cary Grant had it in his contract that no one's name could appear longer than his in any movie advertisement. Coincidentally, Eva Marie Saint, his co-star in *North by Northwest*, had a similar contract clause stipulating that her name had to appear in a certain type size.

The ad agency had quite a problem stretching Cary Grant's name until it was longer than Ms. Saint's.

The first all-talking picture was *The Lights of New York*, directed by Bryan Foy; *The Jazz Singer* only had dialogue in key scenes. A gangster film, most of *The Lights of New York*'s scenes were played into microphones hidden in telephones or flowerpots.

Zecca, the French film pioneer, introduced in the 1890s the first screen flashback in his film *Histoire d'un Crime*—in which a murderer dreams of his past.

FINGERS AND FINGERPRINTS

An unusual aspect of a damages claim in the British High Court in 1975 was that Agyemang Sarkodee claimed that losing parts of three of his fingers in a machine meant he had also lost his kingship.

Mr. Sarkodee's tribe is the Agona clan, which lives around Kwabre in Ghana. His lawyer said: "The basis of the claim is that he would have become king when his uncle retires in two years' time. And because of the tribal custom, no person who has suffered disfigurement can become king."

The first conviction made in Britain on fingerprint evidence was against Harry Jackson, accused of stealing billiard balls from a house in Denmark Hill in June, 1902.

The Argentinian police force was the first to adopt the use of fingerprints to investigate crimes.

Astronaut Neil Armstrong, the first man on the moon, had his ring finger ripped off in November, 1978, when he jumped from his truck at his suburban home near Cincinnati and his wedding band caught on a barn door. A surgical team led by Dr. Joseph E. Kutz restored the finger.

FIRST WORDS

The first—the *very* first—words were probably grunts. However, somewhere between the last ice age and recorded history, possibly at the time when agriculture was being developed, the grunts began turning into words—and it seems to have happened at a specific place and time. All of the world's languages, from Tibetan to Swahili, are now thought to have evolved from small tribes wandering Central Europe about twelve thousand years ago.

The evidence for this lies in common words that occur in every tongue, so similar that they are beyond coincidence. Father, for instance, is *athir* in Irish, *pater* in Latin, *pidar* in Persian, and *pitr* in Sanskrit. Water, which today is *voda* in Russian (*vodka* means "little water") or *wasser* in German, goes right back to *watar* in the biblical language of the Hittites.

Jacob Grimm, coauthor of *Grimm's Fairy Tales*, was one of the detectives who followed the clues back to the first prehistoric language, which they called Indo-European. It has been possible to reconstruct some key words, and these give us a picture of the lives of the Indo-Europeans. They had domesticated sheep or *owa* (ewes) and the *gwou*, which gave them *melg* to drink. They planted *gran*, which was then ground in a *mel*. In due course it was mixed with *wodor* (water) and *yes* (yeast) to make *dheigh* (dough) for *pa* (bread, as in the Latin *panis*). On the spiritual side, they believed in *ghutom* (the first word for God, "the being that is worshipped"), who was *sac* (sacred). Finally, they counted from one to ten, as *oinos, duo, treies, qetwer, pende, sweks, septn, okto, newm, dekm.*

FISH

Angler fish live in the depths of the ocean and are hideous-looking—mostly mouth—with a light-emitting lure dangling from their jaws to attract prey. The light is in fact produced by a colony of symbiotic bacteria, a kind of subcontracted light show; the female angler has a second type of light-emitter powered by her own energy reserves, whose function is to attract the young fish of the species. The young angler is of no particular sex, but once it attaches itself to the head of the female, it turns into a male and remains attached to the female's head as a parasite. Its organs gradually wither away until it is little more than a portable sperm bank with which the female makes new young.

The Atlantic fish is five inches long and has a light in its eyes, which it can switch on and off and use to attract food. First discovered off the coast of Jamaica in 1907, only nine have ever been captured alive.

The cuckoo fish is an African fresh-water fish reared in the mouth of a member of another species, usually the *cichlidae* family of mouth-breeders. The female cichlid will brood her fertilized eggs in her mouth until they hatch, calling the small fry back whenever danger threatens. Among several of the questions puzzling scientists is how the cuckoo, a surface-living plankton-feeder, is transferred to the foster parent, a deep-water predator—and why the *cichlidae* have evolved no means of resisting the parasite.

The flesh of the drummer fish, which lives in the waters around Norfolk Island (off the coast of Australia), is hallucinogenic. Known locally as "dreamfish," eating it gives people bizarre dreams and a paranoid feeling that others are trying to hunt them.

The Brazilian coastal river fish, *Problodus heterostomus*, is the spitting image of another species, *Astyanax fasciatus*, whose scales it eats. The advantage of *Problodus'* disguise is that it can swim undetected in an *Astyanax* shoal and attack its members at will; after an attack, *Problodus* becomes once again just another member of the shoal.

In the mid-1960s, "walking catfish" from Southeast Asia were a novelty in Florida fish farms. About one foot long and weighing a pound, the catfish can (when tired of swimming) hop out of the water and creep along the ground by balancing on its pectoral fins, arching its back, dragging its tail forward, and then flopping out full length.

By 1969, the walking catfish, bored with farm life, had made their way over much of Florida and are now distributed over 3,380 square miles in ten counties. Environmentalists, noting the catfishes' voracious appetites, fear they will denude lakes and ponds throughout the southeastern U.S. Apparently they have already "taken over some good-sized ponds" and, says one Florida Game and Fresh Water Commission member, "they're still walking."

FLAVORS

It is well known that all the colors we see can be broken down into three primaries—yellow, red, and blue—and that it's possible to make any color by combining them. But what about taste? Can one define the primary *flavors*?

Susan Schiffman and Charles Dackis of Duke University, North Carolina, set out to do this scientifically by feeding a variety of basic substances, such as salts and vitamins, to a group of volunteers who were carefully chosen because they had no sense of smell, which could have been confused with the taste. The results were surprising. The primary colors mark out a "triangle" of color-space, and it had always been thought that taste-space had four corners marked "sweet," "sour," "salty," and "bitter." The tests showed that four of the extremes were indeed glycine (sweet), ascorbic acid (sour), quinine hydrochloride (bitter), and sodium chloride (salt), but they also revealed three other basic tastes that fell outside this pattern, which they described as "fatty," "sulphurous," and "alkaline."

They also discovered a relationship between the taste of something and the shape of the molecules of which it was composed. For instance, amino acids with side-chains on their molecules were tasteless, heavy amino-acid molecules were bitter, and lightweight ones were sweet.

FLIGHT

The distance between the wingtips of a Boeing 747 is longer than the first flight made by the Wright Brothers.

Pan Am's first commercial flight was a 90-mile mail run from Key West, Florida, to Havana on October 28, 1927. Fifty years later, to mark the anniversary, a Pan American World Airways Boeing 747 flew around the world via the North and South Poles in 54 hours, 7 minutes, and 12 seconds. On board were 169 passengers, and their in-flight entertainment included 12 films, a fashion show, Maori dancing, and a magician.

Chris English, a flight fanatic, has traveled 405,000 miles to 26 countries on 1,200 flights on 56 different airlines—all for less than $5,000. He once flew 133 times in 15 days on a special $90 plan for foreigners in Finland. In all this flying he has suffered jet lag only once, and lost his baggage (briefly) twice.

In February, 1977, Qantas, the Australian airline, flew the first chartered excursion to the Antarctic and back, taking three hundred people on an eleven-hour, nonstop jumbo jet flight over the South Pole.

The first balloon flight by a human being was made on October 15, 1783, by a young French scientist, Pilatre de Rozier, in a linen-and-paper balloon built by the Montgolfier brothers. But de Rozier was not the first balloonist. A month before, a duck, a sheep, and a rooster had gone aloft for eight minutes, watched by Louis XVI and Marie Antoinette.

Early balloon flights caused a sensation throughout Europe. The *Journal de Bruxelles* reported on a flight in early 1784: "It is impossible to describe that moment: the women in tears; the common people raising their hands toward the sky in deep silence; the passengers, leaning out of the gallery, waving and crying out for joy.... You follow them with your eyes, you call to them as if they could hear, and the feeling of fright gives way to one of wonder. No one said anything but, 'Great God, how beautiful!' Grand military music began to play, and firecrackers proclaimed their glory."

The first play about balloons was staged in London the same year. Entitled *Aerostation*, it concerned the "passion of a lady of fortune for balloons."

Balloons were first used by the military in April, 1794, when the French revolutionary government authorized the formation of the First Company of Balloonists. Qualifications for joining included a special knowledge of chemistry, sketching, carpentry, and masonry.

The sport of aerobatics was founded by Lieutenant Nestorer of the Imperial Russian Air Service, who took his Nieuport monoplane into the sky above Kiev in August, 1913, and looped the loop—an unheard-of thing at the time.

His superiors did not approve of his "death loop," and when he reached the ground, the lieutenant was charged with endangering government property and placed under house arrest for a month.

Neither did he get any glory. His thunder was stolen by Adolph Pegoud, a Frenchman known as "the foolhardy," who had already become the first pilot to parachute from a plane in mid-flight when his Bleriot monoplane stalled at 250 feet. Pegoud looped the loop in a blaze of publicity in September, 1913, and claimed the honors of being the first.

FLOATING ISLAND

In 1969, the U.S. destroyer escort *John D. Pearce* spotted an island sailing independently across the Caribbean, a good sixty miles from the nearest land. The island (probably part of Brazil) was fifteen yards across, with a group of full-sized thirty-five-foot palm trees growing on it, and it was making a good two and a half knots in a westerly direction between Cuba and Haiti. It was later reported missing, believed sunk.

FLU

Common influenza, or flu, has produced ten major and twenty minor pandemics in the last 250 years. It was first described by Hippocrates, the "father" of western medicine, who reported a flu epidemic in the Athenian army in 412 B.C.

The greatest known flu pandemic lasted fifteen months during 1918-19 and took between twenty and forty million lives—more than all those killed in the four years of the First World War. It infected at least one-fifth of the total human population of the time. Called "Spanish flu," it is now believed to have originated in the United States, where it took 550,000 lives. In San Francisco, over a quarter of the 3,500 patients admitted to one hospital died. In the city's streets, people wore gauze facemasks, and the Armistice was greeted by "tens of thousands of deliriously happy, dancing, singing, masked celebrants."

Flu viruses are shaped like sea urchins, with two different kinds of spikes protruding from a spherical body about four-millionths of an inch in diameter. Pandemics are caused by the emergence of new and virulent types of flu virus with altered spikes.

Strains of flu are prevalent in many domestic and wild animals including pigs, horses, calves, dogs, chickens, and turkeys. One type of animal can infect another. Migratory birds are also infected by flu and are thought to be responsible for the geographical spread of different virus strains, transmitting the infection via their droppings.

The ballistics of the flu-spreading human sneeze are: muzzle velocity—103 miles an hour; range—up to twelve feet; density—up to eighty-five million viruses per sneeze.

FOOD

According to *African Insect Recipes* by Martha Wapensky, the correct way to cook the African Fried Flying Ant is as follows: "Fry the ants in a dry pan. Remove the pan, dry the ants in the sun, and winnow out wings and any stones. Fry the ants again, with or without a little oil, add a bit of salt, and cook until done. Serve with rice."

The Chinese eat dogs—stewed, fried, minced, and served with lots of chili.

A gourmet service in England offers, for fifty-five dollars, a dormouse, electrocuted and skinned, which should then be eaten by braising in honey or wine and lightly fried in butter.

There is a live-minnow-eating festival held every year in Geraardsbergen, Belgium. Minnows are dropped into a silver chalice full of red wine, then drunk.

An article in the authoritative medical journal *The Lancet* in September, 1978, reported on the high percentage of people in the poorer rural areas of the southern United States who eat earth and clay. This practice is believed to be beneficial to the bowels—not unreasonable, since Kaopectate and Parapectolin are both made from Kaolin, a type of clay. In 1965, *The Washington Post* reported on widespread consumption in the South of large quantities of laundry starch, particularly by pregnant women.

Chicken feathers are ninety-seven percent protein, and University of Georgia researchers have found a way of turning them into a fine white powder that is said to be easy to digest. A panel who tasted cookies made from this described them as "pretty good to eat."

Every year in Japan, about two hundred people die from eating the fu-gu, a fish considered a delicacy. It has a poison in its guts, and only licensed cooks are allowed to prepare it.

In 1868, a horsemeat banquet for 160 was held at London's Langham Hotel. The highlight of the meal was a 280-pound baron of horse carried on the shoulders of four chefs.

The North American Bait Company once sponsored a "cooking with worms" competition. The winning recipe was for Earthworm Applesauce Surprise Cake.

In 1978, movie director Herb Robbins held a worm-eating competition at Rialto College, California, to promote his movie *The Worm Eaters*. The winner, Rusty Rice, ate twenty-eight.

McDonald's has sold some twenty-five billion hamburgers since the company started. If stacked, they would make twenty piles the height of the Sears Tower in Chicago. The worldwide chain has sold enough milkshakes to fill every gas tank in America.

At its peak, Colonel Sanders' Kentucky Fried Chicken franchises created the fortunes of 125 millionaires. Colonel Sanders is only an honorary colonel, and he doesn't own the company anymore, having sold out his interests in 1964 for two million dollars.

Chewing gum was invented by a photographer called Thomas Adams, who originally planned to use it as a substitute for rubber.

American scientists are developing "nonfood" items that look and taste just like real food but cannot be absorbed by the human body. The idea of "nonfood" is that compulsive eaters will be able to devour large portions of their favorite dishes without putting on an ounce.

Six Russian inventors filed a patent in 1977 describing a method of producing synthetic caviar in fifty-two varieties. The caviar is based on granules of aqueous gelatin containing edible protein.

FORGERY

The most infamous philatelic forger of all time was an Italian, Jean de Sperati, who had an amazing knowledge of photography, printing, and chemistry and, in his lifetime, produced between fifty and seventy thousand of what he termed his "artistic reproductions."

In 1953, when the British Philatelic Association heard that Sperati wanted to pass his knowledge on, it made a deal to buy him out, destroying his machinery and acquiring his reference collection, master blocks, and a typescript describing his methods. The BPA has kept these a closely guarded secret ever since. Sperati died in 1957.

IBM has produced a pen designed to prevent the forging of signatures. The pen includes an "accelerometer," which records the muscular spasms in your hand when you are writing; this recording can then be transferred onto paper as a squiggle on a graph. Everyone displays a unique pattern of muscular spasms when signing his or her name, which is impossible for a forger to reproduce. With the IBM pen, it's not *what* you write but *how you write it* that shows whether the signature is forged or genuine.

FRAUDS

Ptolemy, the Greek astronomer whose theory of an Earth-centered solar system held sway for fourteen hundred years until Copernicus, was a scientific fraud. He claimed that his ideas were derived from observation, but in fact he stole all the figures he needed from another astronomer, Hipparchus, and then changed them all by the same amount to get the results he wanted. The fraud was not revealed until the publication in 1977 of a book by Dr. Robert Newton, because Ptolemy's work was so revered that no one bothered, or dared, to check his supposed observations.

A Bavarian cheesemaker violated local food laws by using a mechanical scoop to cut holes in cheese when the ripening process failed to produce them. The court fined him 300 marks (approx. $166) and declared, "Swiss cheese with mechanically made holes is misleading."

In 1978, the Premier of Thailand sentenced a tapioca exporter to life imprisonment for having sent a shipment to Holland which consisted mainly of gravel. For the record, the man's name was Hua Oathommarutsamaphong.

In 1913, radio pioneer Lee de Forest was tried on a charge of fraud for selling stock in his Radio Telephone Company. "De Forest has said in many newspapers and over his signature that it would be possible to transmit the human voice across the Atlantic before many years," said the district attorney, indignant that anyone could believe such nonsense. "Based on these absurd and deliberately misleading statements," he added, "the misguided public has been persuaded to purchase stocks in his company."

The modern master of defrauding welfare offices is Antonio Moreno, aka the King of Kiddology. In the early 1970s he invented three thousand children for himself over a period of several years, and extracted thirty million francs from the French social security system. He then successfully evaded the authorities and now lives happily in his native Valencia, Spain, from which he cannot be extradited.

During the summer of 1924, a Scottish con man named Arthur Ferguson hoodwinked American tourists into buying Big Ben for £1,000 and Nelson's Column for £6,000, and putting a down payment of £2,000 on Buckingham Palace.

FREAKS

Tripp and Bowen were a famous double act: Tripp had no arms and Bowen had no legs. They used to ride a tandem bicycle together, with Tripp saying, "Bowen, watch your step," and Bowen retorting, "Keep your hands off me."

James Morris had "elastic skin," and could pull the skin of his chest up to the top of his head and stretch his cheeks eight inches out from the side of his face.

Among Barnum and Bailey's Giant American Museum of Human Phenomena and Prodigies were the following: the Poodle Man, who had long silky hair covering his face, eyes, nose, ears, chin, and neck; Alfonso, the Man with the Ostrich Stomach, who could chew up glass and pebbles, swallow nails, eat soap, and wash it all down with gasoline and ammonia; the Telescope Man, a young American who had the ability to lengthen or shorten his spinal column at will, increasing and decreasing his height.

Mac Norton, the Human Aquarium, swallowed (and ejected), three gallons of water and two dozen live frogs.

A seventy-five-year-old woman in Montgomery, Alabama, carried a calcified and almost full-term fetus in her abdomen for twenty-four years without realizing it. The fetus, the result of a rare abdominal pregnancy, was discovered when the woman died during an operation for a gunshot wound received during a family quarrel.

A two-headed baby boy born in Tucuman, Argentina, was given two baptisms because the Catholic Church ruled that each head should be treated as independent. The baby can feed through either mouth and is in good health and mentally alert.

GAMBLING

GANGS

GARBAGE

GARDEN
   ORNAMENT

GEMS

GENERAL
   BAROMETER

GESTURES

GIGS

GLUE

GODS AND THEIR
   PRIESTS

GOLD

GRAVITY

THE GREAT BENGAL
   FROG WAR

GROWTH

GAMBLING

"It's a funny thing—gamblin'. It's like running a grocery store. You buy and you sell. You pay the going rate for cards and you try and sell 'em for more than you paid."
—Pug Pearson, former World Poker Champion

The Horseshoe Casino at Las Vegas (where the World Poker Championships are held) has the world's highest limit at craps and, in the foyer, a large glass-enclosed vault in which a million dollars in cash is displayed.

For years, a pair of dice rested on a velvet cushion in the Desert Inn Casino, Las Vegas. The dice were used by a roller who made an incredible twenty-eight passes at the craps table in June, 1950, against odds of a hundred million to one. Unfortunately, he only bet $2 on each throw and ended with $750 instead of the almost $300 million he would have won if he had let his winnings ride. The dice were lost during rebuilding.

A Spanish royal decree banned civil servants, military men, minors, drunks, madmen, and convicts on parole from gambling casinos.

El Gordo, "the Fat One," is reputed to be the world's richest lottery. In 1973, the total prize money amounted to 1.19 billion pesetas ($133 million). Set up in 1763 by King Carlos III as an additional source of revenue for the Spanish state, it has been held every Christmas ever since.

"The Man Who Broke the Bank at Monte Carlo" was an Englishman, Charles Deville Wells, who sat down at the tables with a £400 stake and emerged three days later with £40,000, which would be worth about $10 million today. His method was simply to go on betting on either red or black, doubling his stake each time he lost. For his time, it was a fairly good system, although had he lost thirty consecutive spins, or "coups," he would have owed the house 1,073,741,823 times his original stake.

However, it was 1891 when Wells broke the bank, and this type of mega-gamble has since been made impossible for two reasons: the right of the house to limit the size of individual stakes, and the existence of zero.

On a roulette wheel, which is divided into eighteen black and eighteen red spaces, the odds of the ball landing on either color are one to one. But every wheel contains an extra space, labeled zero, and if the ball lands in it, all the bets are wiped off the table. This gives the house real odds of one and one-eighteenth to one, which will eventually beat any mathematical system. Just to make sure of their profit margin, there is an additional insurance. Although there are thirty-six numbers, which (with zero) should give the gambler odds of thirty-seven to one, no house will offer better odds than thirty-five to one.

In the long history of the Monte Carlo Casino, no one has beaten a consecutive run of 28 successful coups. The odds are so great against this happening that it has been calculated that a run of 32 wins might be expected once every 50 years from 1,000 true wheels spun 250 times a day.

Wyatt Earp and Casanova were both professional faro players.

Edward Thorp was the first person to discover, mathematically, that blackjack was not primarily a game of chance. Using an IBM 704 computer, he worked out a basic strategy for beating the bank, financed by two anonymous New York businessmen. The first time he tried it, he broke the bank twice in one night at the Wagon Wheel Casino at Lake Tahoe, Nevada, after which the casinos banned him.

Thorp commented: "The people who run casinos are tough and smart in many ways, but they belong to the Dark Ages. I can hardly believe the way their minds work. They explain the phenomena of their world the way the ancient astrologers did. They actually believe the dice get hot."

"There are few things that are so unpardonably neglected in our country as poker. The upper class knows very little about it. Now and then you find ambassadors who have a sort of general knowledge of the game, but the ignorance of the people is fearful. Why, I have known clergymen, good men, kindhearted, liberal, sincere, and all that, who did not know the meaning of a flush. It is enough to make one ashamed of one's species."

—Mark Twain

After the Big Three meetings at Potsdam, President Truman was resting at sea aboard the U.S.S. *Augusta* while he made the fateful decision to drop the atom bomb on Japan. During this time he played poker nonstop with the press, often starting at 8:30 A.M., with a short break for lunch and dinner, and ending around midnight. Some of the reporters in Truman's entourage had to pad their expense accounts for weeks to get their losses back. One of the reporters recalls how he was awakened from bed before 8:00 A.M. and summoned to the president to receive the news of the forthcoming A-bomb explosion over Hiroshima. He said, "Once this graphic secret was told to us for later publication, out came the cards and chips."

GANGS

Manhattan Island in the nineteenth century was a dangerous place, terrorized by such gangs as the Dead Rabbits (Irishmen who fought under a rabbit impaled on a spike), the Plug Uglies, the Molasses Gang (who specialized in ramming a hatful of treacle over their victim's head), the Daybreak Boys (killers aged ten and under), the Swamp Angels (who used the sewer system for raids and escapes), and the Charltons—led by Sadie the Goat.

GARBAGE

James J. Fahey, author of the best-seller *Pacific War Diary*, retired recently from the job he had held before, during, and after the book's success: driving a garbage truck. Fahey, at sixty, had thirty years of rubbish collection behind him, and in 1964 received the "Garbage Man of the Year" award from the U.S. Refuse Disposal Association. Fahey says he's the only holder of that distinction. His book royalties, some $60,000, were sent to a missionary friend to build a church in Mettupattie, India.

The U.S. Court of Appeals for the Seventh Circuit ruled in 1978 that a citizen's right of privacy does not extend to his rubbish. The court issued its opinion to uphold the conviction of Thomas Shelby of Milwaukee on charges of stealing $3,000 in coin from several banks. Mr. Shelby was apprehended when law enforcement officers searched through his trash and came up with coin wrappers and discarded coin trays. The three-judge panel ruled that: "The defendant could not reasonably have believed that the city sanitation department had any responsibility to help him dispose of evidence of his crimes."

GARDEN ORNAMENT

Paul Kay of Solihull, England, has a German fighter plane, a Messerschmitt ME-109, in the front garden of his detached house. It stands on its retractable undercarriage, facing the living room. His wife commented, "We prefer the Messerschmitt to birdbaths. If we want to be eccentric, it is entirely our own affair."

A spokesperson for the Solihull Planning Department said: "There is no regulation to prevent this family from having a German fighter in their garden. I suppose if a lot more people started parking Messerschmitts, then we should have to think about making a new bylaw."

GEMS

According to occult theories of the significance of precious stones:

Agate —will avert violent storms and counteract the sting of scorpions.

Amber	—should be worn when casting enchantments and makes women irresistibly attractive.
Amethyst	—preserves a person from drunkenness and is employed in magical rites to achieve political power and ascendancy over the masses.
Emerald	—symbolizes passionate love, fertility, birth, and reincarnation.
Lapis lazuli	—is the stone of Laz, the Arabian goddess of love; and the sexual organ of Ishtar (the Assyrian Venus) was carved from it.
Onyx	—is used by sorcerers in rituals involving death.
Pearls	—represent purity and virginity.
Ruby	—is associated with Mars and so with warfare, destruction, and blood.
Topaz	—makes its wearers fearless and wise and gives them power over wild beasts. The gem is also a potent remedy against lunacy because it concentrates the sun's rays and so neutralizes the maddening effects of the moon.

GENERAL BAROMETER

In the 1880s, an economist named Alfred de Foville took the statistics for thirty-two unrelated social and economic phenomena (i.e., tobacco sales, suicides, inland revenue, coal output, legacies, etc.) and compiled a barometer on which socially favorable trends were marked in white, unfavorable trends in black, and intermediate trends in different shades of gray. He claimed that at a single glance you could get a good idea of the state of the country's economy. He believed that with this "general barometer," he had founded a new science, which he termed "economic and social meteorology."

GESTURES

Anthropologist Robert A. Bakarat has defined 247 gestures used in the Arab world. When Arabs shake their heads they mean "yes" instead of "no." In Jordan, to flick the right thumbnail against the front teeth means the person making the gesture has no money. Northern Syrians blow smoke into the faces of women they desire. In Libya, the men twist the tips of their forefingers into their cheeks when speaking to beautiful women, while in Saudi Arabia kissing the top of another man's head is a sign of apology. Bakarat claims, "To tie an Arab's hand while he is speaking is tantamount to tying his tongue."

According to Roger Bennet, a journalism professor, the human subconscious produces bizarre facial expressions, particularly rapid eye movement, when the person is lying. He calls these "micromomentaries." They occur at one-sixtieth of a second, far quicker than blinking, which takes one-fifth of a second. Bennet claims, "We know that a psychopathic liar can beat a polygraph, but to the best of my knowledge he can't beat this."

From *A Dictionary of Gestures*, written by Drs. Franz and Betty Bauml after ten years' study: "Probably the most common gesture is the handshake as a sign of greeting. The ancient Greeks used it, and the Romans used to shake hands with statues of Gods for good luck." Thumbing your nose with fingers outstretched is another old and international gesture. It has been dated back to a painting of 1560, and the Baumls think it is older still.

GIGS

Johann Strauss conducted a concert in Boston on July 4, 1872, with twenty thousand musicians and singers on the stage. Strauss gave the beat to no less than one hundred sub-conductors.

A rock promoter once approached the Chilean government with a plan to stage a Rolling Stones concert on Easter Island. Although the island is situated 2,300 miles from the South American coast, the promoter envisaged chartering ships and planes to ferry an estimated 100,000 rock fans to the island for three days. He was turned down.

GLUE

The Romans were the first to produce glue, by boiling down mistletoe juice and then spreading it out on trees to catch birds. Glue has also been produced from blood, milk, potatoes, and bones.

In 1978, the United States used more than forty pounds of glue per person, a total of five million tons worth $1.5 billion.

GODS AND THEIR PRIESTS

Louwrens van Voorthuizen was a Dutch fisherman until 1950, when he declared himself to be God and assembled a small band of devoted followers known as "Lou-men" and "Lou-women." He preached that traditional Christianity was obsolete now that God had returned to Earth, and rejected all forms of conventional morality. He was passionately fond of cigars, and justified his habit with the immortal remark, "Why shouldn't God smoke?" He died in 1968.

The priest of the Roman god Jupiter was called the *flamen* and lived a difficult life. He wasn't allowed to ride a horse, swear an oath, see the army, touch a corpse, or enter a tomb. He couldn't have knots in his clothing or hair, or walk in bowers of vine trees. He couldn't touch or even talk of raw meat, female goats, beans, or ivy. Nor could he eat unleavened bread. He had to have his hair cut by a freeman rather than by a slave, and both his cut hair and his nail parings had to be buried under a fruit tree. He also had to sleep on a bedstead whose feet were smeared with clay, and keep sacrificial cakes in his bedroom.

His priestess wife, the *flaminica*, had to observe all those rules and some extra ones, such as keeping a fruit tree twig in her elaborate headdress and never climbing a ladder beyond the third rung.

Asmodeus, Demon of Lust, rode a dragon, carried a spear, and had the feet of a cock. In the *Testament of Solomon* (c. 100-400 A.D.), he boasts: "My business is to plot against the newly married, so that they may not know one another . . . I transport men into fits of madness and desire when they have wives of their own, so that they leave them and go off by night and day to others that belong to other men with the result that they commit sin."

Asmodeus was originally Aeshma Deva, the Persian "fiend of the wounding spear," a storm spirit personifying rage. Imported from Persia into Palestine as Ashmedai, he provoked rage by causing frustration in marriage. In the *Book of Tobit* (c. 250 B.C.), Sarah has seven husbands, all of whom are strangled by Asmodeus to prevent them from lying with her. Sarah then marries Tobias. On the advice of the angel Raphael, Tobias burns the heart and liver of a fish, and the smoke drives the demon away. In a later version, Tobias and Sarah defeat Asmodeus by voluntarily refraining from sexual intercourse during the first three nights of their marriage. This became the foundation of the custom of "Tobias nights," practiced in parts of nineteenth-century France, Germany, and eastern Europe, in which newlyweds followed their example.

In his book *Strange Sects and Cults*, Egon Larsen records the following:
—the Electricity Culture Religion, who elevated Thomas Alva Edison to the status of a god.
—A sect called the Four Square Gospel, led by Mrs. Aimee Semple MacPherson, an American revivalist prophet of the 1920s. The sect boasted "a brass band bigger

and louder than Sousa's, a female choir bigger and more beautiful than the Metropolitan Opera chorus, and a costume wardrobe comparable to Ziegfeld's."

—The Essene cult, an early variety of Judaism, who worshipped dogs. They believed that there was a King Dog at the time of Christ, and that it died on the day of the Crucifixion. At the end of Christ's thousand-year reign, another King Dog will appear, and with him the Kingdom of Heaven. Departed souls are accompanied on the road to heaven by dogs.

GOLD

A cubic foot of gold weighs half a ton. If all the gold already mined in the world were made into a solid cube, it would be just eighteen yards high and would weigh 157,464 tons.

Nearly all jet planes have windshields coated with a very fine layer of gold, so thin that it's transparent. This is because gold conducts electricity very well and so makes an excellent defroster.

The world's first reported gold-panning competition was held in 1977 in Tankavaara, Finnish Lapland. The winner panned five grams of gold in 5.52 minutes.

GRAVITY

Gravity may be becoming weaker, some cosmologists argue, because of the expansion of the universe and the resulting decrease in the density of its energy. According to Dr. Thomas C. Van Flandern of the U.S. Naval Observatory, who studied twenty years' worth of records, the estimated rate at which gravity is weakening would mean that a person weighing about 140 pounds would lose about one-millionth of the weight of a paperclip each year.

THE GREAT BENGAL FROG WAR

The incident that later became known as the Great Bengal Frog War actually took place in a jungle clearing outside the Malaysian seaport of Sungai Siup. It began on November 8, 1970, with a small skirmish involving about fifty frogs, but within hours hundreds and then thousands of other frogs joined in. The following day the ground was covered with over ten thousand animals tearing and clawing at each other, and by the end of the week, most of them were dead or had fought themselves to a standstill.

Biologists investigating the phenomenon eventually decided that the creatures had been making love rather than war, and that the event had been in the nature of a mass orgy. Although they are rare occurrences, similar battles had been reported before, and local people looked upon them as bad omens. They had presaged disaster in 1969, when the frogs had appeared just two days before serious Malay-Chinese race riots had broken out. Coincidence or not, the day after the 1970 frog war ended, a gigantic cyclone roared up the Bay of Bengal and struck nearby East Pakistan, killing half a million people in one of the worst natural disasters ever recorded.

GROWTH

In the womb, we increase 240 times in length and over a million times in weight. Even after it is born, a baby doubles its weight every six months. If this growth rate were maintained through maturity, a thirty-year-old adult human would weigh three billion tons.

But compared to other natural growth phenomena, this is trifling. A type of seaweed called giant kelp grows at the rate of half a meter a day, while baby whales put on weight at an astonishing ten pounds an hour.

If a cholera bacterium is put in a test tube of the right nutrients, it will start multiplying within half an hour. At the end of a twelve-hour period, it will have produced *sixteen million* offspring.

HAIL

Hail is produced only in thunderstorms. Ice crystals fall from the top of the cloud, passing through alternate layers of warm and cold air, which melt and re-freeze them. At each stage they accumulate more ice and grow in size. They are bounced up and down through layers of cold and warm air, until eventually their weight becomes great enough for them to fall through the updrafts. A weird demonstration of this process occurred in 1930, when five German glider pilots bailed out in a stormcloud high above some mountains. The updraft of the wind carried them right to the top of the cloud. Only one survived. The other four arrived on the earth as human hailstones, frozen to death.

During a severe hailstorm at Vicksburg, Pennsylvania, on May 11, 1894, a large hailstone was found to have a solid nucleus consisting of a piece of alabaster. During the same storm, at a location some eight miles east of Vicksburg, a gopher turtle, measuring six by eight inches and entirely encased in ice, fell with the hail.

HAIR . . . AND LACK OF IT

The winner of the *National Enquirer's* longest-hair competition was Mary Tucker of Long Beach, California, whose seventy-eight-and-a-half-inch locks are eleven inches longer than she is tall.

Nurse Irena Godyn has the longest hair in Britain—seventy-six inches long. When she washes it, she has to use a whole bottle of shampoo and the complete length of her bathtub.

A Scottish hairdresser named Melvin Wood created the world's first tartan hairstyle, called "The Kilt," in twenty hours, using twenty-two colors—at a cost of $220.

There have only been two bald Presidents—Martin van Buren and Dwight Eisenhower.

The Razor's Edge is a bimonthly magazine devoted to "exploring bald-headedness as a legitimate female hair-style ... As beauty. As erotica. As protest. As a political statement." The first issue, published in 1977, featured a bald-headed version of Farrah Fawcett-Majors.

According to a report by New York researcher George de Leon, academics, businessmen, shopkeepers, and other groups of men are more likely to go bald than winos—proving the theory that alcohol prevents baldness.

HANDEDNESS

An average of 90.8 percent of people are right-handed. This proportion is believed to have remained the same for thousands of years. Two Canadian psychologists who examined the incidence of left- and right-handedness in thousands of ancient wall and pottery paintings, statues, and carvings, found that 92.6 percent of our forebears were right-handed. The lack of any significant geographical variation suggests that handedness is inherited, not learned.

HEADLINES

Language does not have to be long-winded to be effective. Bernard Shaw, for instance, made literature out of his one-line postcards, and newspaper headlines and graffiti can be art forms in their own right.

The London *Times* journalist, Claude Cockburn, won a competition among his colleagues for the Most Boring Headline with the classic: SMALL EARTHQUAKE IN CHILE—NOT MANY DEAD, but the truly immortal examples are the real headlines that conveyed such startling (if unintended) information as: MACARTHUR FLIES BACK TO FRONT, or BRITISH PUSH BOTTLES UP GERMANS, which announced respectively that the general had returned to Korea and that an Allied advance in World War II had trapped the enemy. Sometimes they achieve a mysticism that touches on poetry as in: WRONG MAN JUMPS FROM WINDOW.

"The Gunfight at the O.K. Corral" was originally reported on page three of the *Tombstone Epitaph*, a local Arizona newspaper, under the headline: THREE MEN HURLED INTO ETERNITY IN THE DURATION OF A MOMENT.

HEART

The heart must be one of the most efficient machines in existence: a self-repairing reciprocal pump circulating blood through sixty thousand miles of flexible tubing, from arteries an inch in diameter to capillaries so fine that ten of them are no thicker than a hair. It is self-regulating, with a built-in electrical timing device running off a chemical battery and accurate to within 1/50,000th of a second. It can vary its output from five to twelve gallons a minute, directing it to different parts of the system as required, pumping the equivalent of one and a half million gallons a year or, during a lifetime, enough blood to fill the fuel tanks of a fleet of 2,100 Boeing 747 jets.

HEIGHT

The ruler of Gabon is President Albert Bernard Bongo who, because he is under five feet tall, wears platform shoes and has forbidden anyone in his country from using the word "pygmy." He rides around in a silver Cadillac ambulance, and one Western reporter described his palace as "part James Bond movie, part *Star Trek*."

People grow taller when they are asleep. The disks in the spinal column act like sponges. During the day they are subjected to high pressure and liquid is squeezed out, but when you lie down at night the liquid is reabsorbed, making the spine longer and adding up to a third of an inch to your height.

The same phenomenon explains why astronauts who have experienced long periods of weightlessness may return to Earth as much as two inches taller than when they blasted off.

On the other hand, with old age the spine loses its spongelike elasticity, and as a result old people tend to shrink, losing as much as three inches compared to their height during their youthful heyday.

HELA CELLS

Tissue culture is the art of persuading human body cells to grow in glass containers for purposes of biomedical research.

It all started in 1951, with a strain of cells known as HeLa. HeLa cells reproduced so rapidly that, according to one journal: "If allowed to grow uninhibited under optimal culture conditions, they would have taken over the world by this time."

HeLa cultures are all derived from one tiny piece of the flesh of a thirty-one-year-old black woman, Helen Lane, who died of cancer of the cervix in Baltimore in 1951. Her cells proved to be a phenomenon—not just dependable, but positively aggressive. Though it took scientists some twenty years to realize it, HeLa cells were infecting and taking over other tissue cultures, thereby rendering suspect an entire body of scientific research.

No wonder the men's room at a medical school library in San Francisco has a graffito reading: HELEN LANE LIVES.

THE HERO SHREW

The hero shrew, *Scutisorex*, has an unusual spine with bony knobs on it that are designed to prevent the animal from being crushed when it burrows under rocks and boulders. So strong is this backbone that the tiny animal is said to be able to bear the weight of a 170-pound man and survive the ordeal without injury.

HIBERNATION

Hibernation is one of physiology's most baffling tricks. Wild bears, for instance, can sleep for up to five months without once eating, drinking, urinating, or defecating. For about a month before going into winter sleep, the bear is ravenous, eating twenty hours a day and gaining more than a hundred pounds. The bear's temperature during hibernation drops by only four degrees, which is why the bear sleeps quite lightly and is liable, if disturbed, to charge any intruder.

Other hibernating animals, like woodchucks, ground squirrels, and many reptiles, experience a drop in temperature of more than sixty degrees. They sleep so soundly that they can be picked up and tossed about without awakening.

HIP HIP HOORAY!

"Hip hip hooray!" was the battle cry of the Crusaders in the Middle Ages. "Hip" or "hep" stood for their slogan *Hieroslyma est perdita*—"Jerusalem is fallen"—and "hooray" is derived from the Slavic curse *Hu-raj*, meaning "To Paradise!" with which the nonbelievers were dispatched.

HIROSHIMA

In 1945, Professor Shogo Nagaoka, a geologist at the University of Hiroshima, collected 6,542 fragments of rubble from beneath the epicenter of the first atom bomb dropped in warfare and calculated the exact height at which it had been detonated by using trigonometry and the heat shadows etched onto stones by the blast. This information was unknown to the Japanese as the Americans had kept all the details of the bomb a strict secret.

The A-bomb explosion caused a flourish of mountain flowers never before seen in Hiroshima. The seeds had been baked into bricks with red mountain clay years before. The bomb blast reduced the bricks to dust, and the heat germinated the seeds.

Just before the *Enola Gay* dropped the A-bomb, copilot Robert A. Lewis wrote in his log: "There will now be a short intermission while we bomb our target." The log was sold in 1978 for $93,000—a record price for an American autographed document.

It's a Pleasure, filmed in Technicolor and starring Sonja Henie and Michael O'Shea, was screened for members of the U.S. 509th composite group on Tinian Island to welcome back pilots from the first A-bomb raid.

A piece of Japanese paper found one and a half miles from the center of the blast had written characters in black ink neatly burned out, while the paper remained unscorched.

A shirt of alternate light and dark gray stripes survived the A-bomb radiation intact only where the light stripes covered the material. One mile from the explosion's epicenter, a woman wearing a white cotton blouse with pale pink sleeves patterned with small sprays of green leaves and red flowers, each three-sixteenths of an inch in diameter, suffered severe burns only where the red flowers had smoldered earlier than the green leaves. The flash point of black cotton is thirty degrees Celsius lower than white cotton.

Immediately after the explosion, a Japanese pilot, two miles from the epicenter, managed to fly his aircraft despite the banana shape of its heat-contorted fuselage; the nose and tail were ten degrees out of alignment.

Around an hour after the drop, black raindrops as big as marbles fell on the city center and lasted for just under two hours—the result of the vaporization of moisture in the fireball and subsequent condensation in the cloud that developed from it.

HITLER

In his youth, Hitler took a room in the apartment of a tailor named Popp at No. 34 Schleissheimer Strasse in Munich. Lenin once lived at No. 106.

Hitler was a great art "collector." In one repository at Alt-Aussee, a salt mine used since the fourteenth century, he had 6,755 works of the old masters stored by the end of the war. These included paintings by Leonardo da Vinci, Michelangelo, Rubens, Rembrandt, and Vermeer. From his bunker Hitler ordered that they should all be blown up— but the order was never carried out.

He did not swim, never got in a rowboat or mounted a horse.

Not a single personal letter of Hitler's exists.

One of Hitler's social pleasures was to hold three-to-four-hour screenings of his favorite films, described by one biographer as "social comedies with insipid wit and sentimental endings."

One of Hitler's personal physicians, Professor Morell, used to give him so many injections that Goering suggested that Morell be dubbed "Reich Injection Master." Hitler was once described as dismissing visitors in the manner "of a person who has just given himself a morphine injection."

During his time in his twenty-room bunker, all of Hitler's documents had to be typed out for him in letters three times normal size on special "Führer typewriters."

HOLDUPS

Drawing a pistol from her handbag, Charlene Zuver held up a supermarket in Santa Ana, California, demanding money from the man behind the counter. This proved difficult as he was Korean and spoke very little English. Eventually he understood and handed her twenty-five dollars, but then drew a pistol from the till and set off in pursuit.

Out in the street, Ms. Zuver hailed a cab but the driver screeched to a halt and jumped out with his hands in the air. She turned around to find herself face to face with the armed Korean. It was some time before each realized that the other was carrying a toy pistol.

In a last desperate effort, Ms. Zuver flagged down a passing car. It was full of plainclothes police on undercover patrol who obliged by giving her a ride—to the city jail.

A supermarket thief in Brooklyn fared little better. After the raid, police were left holding a wooden leg complete with white sock and black suede shoe. The thief didn't get far.

Cashiers at a bank in Nice were slightly amused when a middle-aged woman with a toy gun threatened to burn down the bank with a blowtorch unless they handed over ten thousand francs. They laughed hysterically when she pounded the pistol on the counter and it broke into pieces. The woman, a mother of six, was led away by unsmiling policemen.

After a thirty-one-day trial, during which the jury took seventy-two and a half hours to reach its verdict, a careless crook was sentenced to fourteen years. Alan Wells had been caught for one simple reason. He had only one eye, and when he robbed the bank, he forgot to cut a second eye hole in his mask.

In 1972, a man walked into a California bank with a water pistol and handed the cashier a note that read, "Milk, loaf of bread, pick up laundry." After he panicked and ran, his car wouldn't start.

HOLES

Richard Dunning, a British art director, paid an unknown sum to buy a hole ninety feet deep and three hundred feet wide from a French farmer in 1977. Mr. Dunning claims the hole he owns is historic, having been created by British sappers using sixty tons of dynamite on July 1, 1916—the first day of the Battle of the Somme.

HORSES AND HORSEPOWER

J. C. Williams of South Carolina is one of the largest breeders of miniature horses in the world. He owns more than 150 of them, none taller than thirty-four inches. They sell for around two thousand dollars.

After the Battle of Waterloo in 1815, the then Duke of York had a corridor of his home—Oaklands, in Surrey—lined with the teeth of horses killed in the battle.

In 1850, an Italian engineer invented and built the world's first and last horse-driven locomotive. Called the *Impulsoria,* it comprised a railway carriage surmounted by a treadmill with four plodding horses. Even more curious was the horse-driven shaving machine, which can claim to have been the first powered razor. Up to sixty users at a time could press their bristles to orifices behind which rotated horse-driven cutthroat razors.

HOSPITALS

One of the world's most unusual hospitals is located six hundred feet below ground in an ancient Polish salt mine. Here patients suffering from respiratory diseases spend up to four hours a day breathing air laced with salt and iodine, which stays at a constant seventy degrees Fahrenheit. The Polish Academy of Sciences claims the hospital has a sixty percent recovery rate.

A fish hospital in Japan is believed to be the only one of its kind in the world. Common ailments among its patients are "white spot," "pop-eye," "gill flukes," and "anchor worms." Lack of balance caused by overeating is also a regular problem.

According to Mr. Kataoka, a trained zoologist at the hospital: "If you show fish that you care, they really respond marvelously."

The world's largest (and only?) camel hospital was set up by the Israeli government in 1978. The million-dollar clinic provides a full veterinary service, including X-rays and blood tests, for the twenty thousand Bedouin camels of the Negev desert.

HOW TO BECOME A FAMOUS INVENTOR

Considering the history of discoveries and inventions, certain techniques seem more profitable than others. These are a few of the basic rules:

Stay at home. It is fruitful ground for discoveries, and James Watt's teakettle was not the only domestic insight to change the world. The pneumatic tire was invented by a Scottish vet, John Dunlop, while trying to fix his child's tricycle. The doughnut came into being when a New England schoolboy, Hanson Gregory, suggested to his mother that her rather lumpy cakes would taste better with the centers removed.

Encourage accidents. From Archimedes' bathwater to Newton's apple, the combination of a lucky accident and a sharp mind has often brought results. When a bottle fell off the shelf of his Paris laboratory, a scientist called Benedictus became curious. He noticed that although the bottle had broken, it still retained its shape. It had originally contained a solution of collodion which had evaporated, leaving behind a thin film of cellulose that held the splinters together. He had accidentally invented the safety glass now used in cars.

But for an accident at a nineteenth-century English paper mill, we would never have had blotting paper. A batch of paper had been spoiled by not having the surface properly glazed with size. Before he threw it out, the mill owner tried writing on it, found that the ink was absorbed, and realized its potential.

Please yourself. Don't worry about other people's problems; solve your own, like society debutante Mary Phelps Jacob—who invented the brassiere in 1914 because she found corsets uncomfortable.

Never wash up. Keep things as untidy as possible and never, never throw your old junk out. If Sir Alexander Fleming had washed down his sample dishes, he would not have discovered penicillin. And if the saucemakers Lea and Perrin had not kept some old jars of unsuccessful mixtures in their store, they might not have come to taste one of these unpalatable failures and discovered that several months of maturing had turned it into the delicious, and now legendary, Worcestershire Sauce.

Above all, improvise. Don't worry about having the right materials, just make do with what you have. Chicken Marengo was invented one evening in 1800, just after Napoleon's troops had won a battle outside the northern Italian province of Piedmont. The emperor was hungry, but the only foodstuffs that a foraging party could come up with were a small hen, three eggs, four tomatoes, and six crayfish. They were cooked in oil with a little garlic and served with bread and a nip of brandy, and a military victory gave birth to a culinary triumph. Napoleon was so pleased with the results that he ordered the meal to be served after every battle.

Cigarettes are another result of inspired improvisation,

this time by Napoleon's enemies. A group of Turkish soldiers defending Acre against the French in 1799 had their
communal hookah pipe destroyed by cannonfire and
started rolling their tobacco in the touch-papers used for
firing their guns.

THE HUMAN AQUARIUM

In some ways our bodies are like complicated, mobile
aquariums, because the main liquid in them is not blood,
but water. Each of us has about ten gallons of it sloshing
around inside us, providing the medium for our chemical
signaling system and an inland sea housing billions of
independent organisms, cells, and bacteria that live and
breed in us (and in a real sense *are* us).

The water makes up sixty percent of the weight of the
aquarium, but it also contains enough phosphorus to coat
the heads of 220 matches, sufficient fat for six cakes of soap,
the amount of carbon in twenty-eight pounds of coke, and
about as much iron as there is in a one-inch nail.

HUMAN HEAT

A healthy body has a range in temperature of twelve
degrees Celsius, ranging from the warmest spot—between
the eyes and the nose—to the fingers and toes, which are
coldest.

Long-distance runners have lower body temperatures
than other people. This difference is only about half a
degree Celsius, but this may be enough to help win a race.
One of the major limits to an athlete's endurance is over-
heating. At a certain critical temperature his body simply
ceases to function, whether he wants it to or not. A body
temperature just one-tenth of a degree lower can put off
this critical point for as long as six minutes. And as anyone
who has watched some of the heartrending last laps
around athletic tracks will know, six minutes can make a
great deal of difference.

A hot drink really does make you cooler than an ice-cold one. British scientists used infrared thermography to picture temperature gradients in the body and found that a cold drink only produced local cooling around the mouth. A cup of hot tea, on the other hand, caused an overall drop in skin temperature of one to two degrees Celsius for up to fifteen minutes.

Another common myth bit the dust when the *Journal of Applied Psychology* published a report showing that cold showers actually *increase* sexual arousal. On the other hand, a sauna has the opposite effect! It not only increases the specific gravity and diastolic pressure of the blood, but can produce heart flutter.

English police cadet Andrew Gedge, eighteen, got so hot on a training walk that his temperature reached 106 degrees Fahrenheit, and his blood began to coagulate. He was rushed to the hospital in a coma. One doctor said, "His blood was more or less boiling when he came in." Gedge was saved by being placed in hundreds of pounds of ice collected from hotels and cold stores in the Welsh town of Aberystwyth.

THE HUMAN HEDGEHOG

Jens Kjaer Jenslon has become known as "the human hedgehog" in his native Denmark, and his agonizing problems have secured him a place in medical history.

It all began when Jens, then fifty-seven, was cutting his hedge of spiky barberry bushes. He piled the cut branches in a heap, tripped, fell on them, and was pierced by thousands of inch-long thorns.

He then spent the next six months in the hospital having six thousand thorns removed. But still more deeply embedded thorns kept working their way out, and over the next six years Jens returned to the hospital 248 times.

He has now had a total of 32,131 thorns removed—not counting the ones he pulled out himself at home.

HYENAS

Aristotle said that hyenas lured dogs to their death by imitating the sound of a man vomiting. Bartholomew, a sixteenth-century writer, said hyenas approached houses at night and mimicked the human voice, and even called the people by name so as to lure them out and devour them. In Africa, hyenas were widely regarded as one of the disguises used by magicians and sorcerers. Magicians in Abyssinia were reported to have turned themselves into hyenas in full view of many people, and a story from the Sudan tells how a soldier who had shot a hyena followed its trail of blood to a hut in which he found a magician dying from a fresh wound.

ICE

After years of steady shrinkage, the world's glaciers have been expanding since 1965—a phenomenon that glaciologists explain as part of a regular 150-200-year cycle due to sudden changes in climate. In Norway, the Folgefonna glaciers put on an extra six feet of ice in 1975 alone, while in the Pamir mountains in central Asia, moving glaciers have threatened to engulf two hydroelectric power stations. Another dropped a six-hundred-foot-long, two-million-cubic-meter chunk of ice onto a highway. Fortunately, no vehicles were beneath it at the time.

The largest iceberg on record measured two hundred miles by sixty miles, and had a total area larger than Belgium.

The idea of towing icebergs to Arabia as a source of fresh water is not entirely new. Erasmus Darwin—English physician, inventor, poet, and grandfather of Charles Darwin—suggested in 1792 in his scientific epic poem, *The Economy of Vegetation*, that icebergs should be navigated into tropical waters to reduce extremes of temperature.

John von Neumann, one of this century's most original mathematicians, had the idea of dyeing the polar icecaps and so decreasing the energy they would reflect. The result would have warmed the Earth and made Iceland's present climate like that of Hawaii.

In the nineteenth century, ice from North American ponds was exported commercially to India.

I.D. CARDS

Plans to introduce new identity cards in Kenya ran into an unexpected difficulty: Moslem women refused to be photographed on the grounds that it was against their religion to unveil themselves during the day.

ILLUMINATI

The Order of the Illuminati, or "enlightened ones," was founded in 1776 by Adam Weishaupt, a professor of law at the University of Ingolstadt in Bavaria. Members were graded into Novices, Minervals, and Illuminated Minervals. The order was anticlerical and politically progressive, but its most distinctive feature was the mutual espionage and informing which its members practiced on each other. They had to complete and give to Weishaupt every month a detailed "intelligence report" describing what they knew about the other members. The order was banned by the Bavarian authorities in 1784, many members were arrested, and Weishaupt himself fled abroad. It was revived in 1906 in Berlin and, more recently, in the science fiction trilogy *The Illuminati*, which suggests that the order is at the center of an age-old global conspiracy.

IMITATIVE MAGIC

In 1324, a magician named John of Nottingham made an experimental wax-and-clay model of a courtier, Richard de Sowe. He drove a pin made of lead two inches into the figure's forehead, and caused the real de Sowe to fall into a "raving and shrieking condition." After a month of this, John pulled the pin out of the model's head and stuck it into the model's heart; de Sowe died the same day.

In 1814, Caroline of Brunswick made wax figures of her husband, the Prince Regent. She gave them horns, stuck pins through them, and then put them in the fire to roast and melt. The prince lived on unaffected, and became King George IV of England.

In 1900, a model of President McKinley, pierced by many pins, was burned on the steps of the United States Embassy in London.

In 1939, it was reported from Cairo, Illinois, that "a sure way to kill a man is to place his picture under the eaves at the corner of your house during rainy weather and let the water pour upon it."

INDEXES

The index of the 1978 edition of *Benn's Press Directory* contains, under Women's Interests, ninety magazine titles and cross-references to "children, food, and cookery, health and hygiene, home interests, motherhood, etc." Under the entry Male Interest, there is just one cross-reference: "Sex Interests."

One of the most absurd indexes was for an obscure book called *The Origin of the Human Reason* by St. George Mivart. On page 136, Mivart refers to a speaking parrot—an anecdote that gave the indexer the opportunity of a lifetime:

Absurd tale about a cockatoo, 136
Anecdote, absurd one, about a cockatoo, 136
Bathos and a cockatoo, 136
Cockatoo, absurd tale concerning one, 136
Discourse held with a cockatoo, 136
Incredibly absurd tale of a cockatoo, 136
Invalid cockatoo, absurd tale about, 136
Mr. R——and a tale about a cockatoo, 136
Preposterous tale about a cockatoo, 136
Questions answered by a cockatoo, 136
R——Mr., and a tale about a cockatoo, 136
Rational cockatoo as asserted, 136
Tale about a rational cockatoo, as asserted, 136
Very absurd tale about a cockatoo, 136
Wonderfully foolish tale about a cockatoo, 136

This is all the more astonishing as the book is a very dull one.

INFLATION

Two years after General Pinochet's coup d'etat in Chile in September, 1973, rice in the country had risen in price by 21,027 percent, milk by 17,566 percent, and sugar by 17,400 percent. In one month the cost of living rose 212 percent.

INFORMATION

The most (mechanically) compressed information in the world is probably an experimental system now being developed for computers, which stores ten billion "bits" of information optically on a three-hundred-centimeter plastic disk. Looking exactly like a standard LP, each record contains the equivalent of fifteen volumes of the *Encyclopedia Britannica*, including diagrams and figures.

But technology is crude compared to nature. The cortex of the human brain, which is about 0.1 inches thick by 400 square inches (when it is fully unfolded), records every conscious aspect of a human personality, every sensation, thought, and memory of a whole lifetime.

INSECTS

Insects outnumber and outweigh us. There are more insects in ten square miles of Arctic tundra than there are mammals in all of North America.

The leap of the common flea is one of the wonders of nature. When it jumps, it is as if a kneeling man had leapt to the top of the Post Office tower in London thirty thousand times without tiring. Its acceleration has been measured at twenty times the rate at which a moon rocket escapes Earth's atmosphere.

Cockroaches that have been beheaded can survive for up to seven days because of clusters of nerve cells in other parts of their bodies. Indeed, according to biologists at Michigan State University, the headless cockroaches can be conditioned to avoid painful electric shocks more rapidly than those that still have their heads.

When a supermarket in East Osaka, Japan, offered a bounty of 3.8 cents for a dead cockroach, residents killed 98,499 in a week—a total payout of $3,743. Two women caught 1,351 solely in their apartment house.

The Vietnamese, however, think it is bad luck to kill cockroaches.

Many butterflies and moths have elaborate "eye spots" on their wings in imitation of the eyes of birds of prey. These spots deter small birds from preying on them, but in many species the trick of "wing flashing" serves a dual purpose. The beating of the wings also produces an ultrasonic click that deters another predator, the bat. So effective is this sonic weapon that many bats startle, scream, and fly away from the sound.

How do you sex a glowworm? By studying the flashes of light they emit. Male glowworms emit a pulse of light every 5.8 seconds, females every 2.1 seconds.

The nocturnal sand scorpion can locate its prey in total darkness at a distance of fifty centimeters. It achieves this feat by using tiny hairs and bristles on its eight legs to sense seismic waves sent through the earth by the movements of other insects or animals. By analyzing the direction from which the waves come and the time delay between their reaching his separate legs, the scorpion computes the precise distance and direction of its prey.

The harvestman spider knows what to do when under attack. It detaches one of its eight legs as a distraction to the predator, while making off at top speed on the remaining seven. To make the distraction more convincing, the discarded leg begins to twitch and wriggle as soon as it is detached.

Dragonflies' compound eyes consist of 28,000 lenses providing 200 degrees of vision. They fly at 24 miles an hour, and one Australian specimen was timed at 61.3 miles an hour over a short distance.

Ticks—disease-spreading parasites—suck blood and grow from three to twelve millimeters, and can survive starvation for up to five years. They feed for ten days, copulate for seven, and then the female lays between two thousand and eight thousand eggs. Ticks have been known to live for twenty-five years.

The lacewing is an insect that preys on the woolly alder aphid, so called because it produces a white, waxy covering that looks like wool. These aphids travel about in "flocks" that are shepherded by ants, who are rewarded for their protection with offerings of aphid honeydew. Lacewing larvae, however, infiltrate the aphid flocks and steal the "wool" from the aphids to disguise themselves; with this protection, they are able to ravage the flock unchallenged by the guardian ants.

INSURANCE

Major American insurance companies rate astronauts as their top risks, followed by test pilots, stuntmen, toreadors, hot-air balloonists, lion tamers—and trapeze artists who perform without nets.

George Armstrong Custer, at the time a lieutenant-colonel took out a $5,000 life insurance policy shortly before the Battle of the Little Bighorn.

In 1965, four amateur archaeologists managed to get a $22,000 insurance policy against a death curse, threatened against all who interfered with some mysterious stone circles in Gambia they were planning to investigate.

An Italian whose daughter was leaving home to work in Germany insured her virginity for a capital sum of $1,283.

INTERSTELLAR ANIMALS

A great many more insects and animals than human beings have gone into space. The first fish in space was a group of South American guppies that spent forty-eight days in a zero-gravity aquarium on board the Russian Salyut 5 space station in 1976. There was a large international selection of mice and flies on the Cosmos 936 flight in September, 1977, and other arkloads of creatures, including spiders, were on earlier U.S. bio-satellites from 1969 onward. Dogs were used (and sacrificed) by the Russians in their pioneer space experiments in the same way that chimpanzees were used by the Americans.

INTESTINES

Japanese women who envy the color of Western skin are paying around $1100 to have up to fifty inches of large intestine removed. According to Dr. Tadao Yagi, a Tokyo surgeon: "Medical researchers have discovered that we have much bigger large intestines than white people," and he is convinced that this produces the yellow hue in Japanese people. In most cases, the skin pales less than a week after surgery.

Ancient Mesopotamians used to read the future from the intestines of animals, and seers claimed they could judge the position of an animal's intestines by its appearance. This tradition was continued in the Roman culture by a very specialized group of priests called *haruspices*—inspectors of sacrifices or entrails.

INVENTORS AND INVENTIONS

Coin-operated slot machines were invented by Hero of Alexandria less than a century after Christ, to be used as holy-water dispensers.

The water closet was invented by an amateur poet and godson of Queen Elizabeth I. It was called the Ajax, worked by means of leather valves, and the Queen was so impressed when she tried it out at the inventor's country seat that she immediately ordered one for herself.

Other amateur inventors include King C. Gillette, a traveling cork salesman from Boston, who invented the safety razor. The snapshot camera and roll film were invented by a bookkeeper, George Eastman, who chose the name Kodak in 1888 because it was "short, vigorous, could not be misspelt, and, to satisfy trademark laws, meant nothing." The dial telephone was invented by an undertaker, and a French monk invented the principle of hermetically sealed refrigeration.

John Walker Carlson, who invented xerography, and Einstein, who discovered relativity, were a patent lawyer and a patent clerk respectively.

When James Hetherington, inventor of the top hat, first wore it in public in 1797, he was arrested for causing a breach of the peace.

Chester Greenwood, born in 1877, inventor of the earmuff, also held 125 patents on such devices as a spring-tooth rake, airplane shock absorbers, and self-priming spark plugs.

To celebrate the occasion of his centenary in 1977, his hometown of Farmington, Maine, built a pair of giant earmuffs as big as automobile tires and mounted them on the municipal fire truck, conducted an earmuff fashion show, a "longest ears" competition, and a footrace to the former site of Greenwood's Ear Protector Factory.

Mr. George Rhodes, secretary of the Society of Inventors in Manchester, England, has invented an open-ended trouser rack, a roulette dartboard, and a warm toilet seat cover, which folds away to carry in a handbag.

Thomas Edison fitted his newfangled lightbulbs on the busts of Broadway showgirls and onto the end of Sir Arthur Sullivan's baton—so that he could conduct in the dark.

Procter & Gamble patented a baby's diaper that self-inflates when wetted, thus simultaneously increasing its absorption capacity and alerting mothers to the need for a diaper change.

"Cat's eyes"—reflector studs set in the middle of roads—were invented by an Englishman, Percy Shaw. Though he became a millionaire, he lived a simple life in a house beside his factory in Yorkshire. He had no carpet in his living room so that he could throw onto the floor the continuous stream of matches he used to light his pipe, which he filled with broken-up cigars. He died in 1976, aged eighty-six.

The safety pin was invented by Walter Hunt in 1849, to pay off a debt of fifteen dollars. It took him just three hours.

Unusual inventions registered at the U.S. Patent Office include a strip of silk tape for covering the mouth to stop breathing, registered in 1920 by Richard Jefferies; a tongue shield designed to stop the taste of unpleasant medicines; and a machine designed in 1929 to produce artificial dimples in the cheeks with the aid of three bullet-shaped screws.

When Walter Diemer invented bubble gum in 1928, everyone told him the idea was crazy. Now it's a 140-million-dollar-a-year industry, and Walter is happily retired. But why is bubble gum pink? Walter claims, "Because it was the only coloring I had at the time."

It's becoming too expensive and bothersome to patent devices nowadays, and many inventors have found ways around the bureaucratic process. The electronics industry, for example, "pots" new components in epoxy. If a competitor tries to dissolve the epoxy to learn trade secrets, the solvent destroys key parts of the hidden circuitry. In electronics, the field is moving so rapidly that a new invention can become obsolete before the completion of the patenting process, which can take several years. In addition, it takes thousands of dollars to obtain a patent and often costs $50,000 to enforce it through the courts.

JIFFY   JINXED SHIPS
JUNGLES

JIFFY

A "jiffy" is scientifically defined as a length of time equal to one one hundred thousand billion billionths of a second.

JINXED SHIPS

The 27,000-ton battle cruiser *Scharnhorst* was one of the prides of Hitler's navy, but right from the start she was jinxed by bad luck. While under construction, the ship rolled on her side and killed sixty-one workmen. The night before she was launched in front of Hitler and other top Nazis, the *Scharnhorst* broke her support cables and launched herself, destroying several boats in her path. After war broke out, she attacked the defenseless city of Danzig, but nine of her crew were blown up when one gun exploded, and eleven others suffocated when they were trapped in a gun turret without ventilation. When the *Scharnhorst* limped home after being severely hit during the siege of Oslo, she collided with and sank the S.S. *Bremen*, one of the largest liners of the time. She was repaired and sent north to attack an Allied convoy, but was attacked instead by the Royal Navy and sunk. Out of her crew of eighteen hundred, only thirty-six survived, and two of the survivors died after they swam ashore and tried to light their emergency oil heater—which blew up in their faces.

In 1898, an American author named Morgan Robertson, who wrote his novels in a trancelike state of consciousness, published *The Wreck of the Titan*, a book that describes the tragic maiden voyage of the largest luxury liner ever built, the unsinkable *Titan*. Seventy-five thousand tons dead-weight, she had three propellers, a top speed of twenty-five knots, and carried 2,000–3,000 passengers. But she only had twenty-four lifeboats, far too few to accommodate all the passengers, and on a foggy night in April she crashed into, and was sunk by, a massive iceberg.

The *Titanic* was built thirteen years later; she also displaced 75,000 tons, had three screws and a maximum speed of twenty-five knots. She was "the largest craft afloat" and had the same reputation for invulnerability. On her maiden voyage in 1912, the *Titanic* sank after encountering an iceberg on the night of April 14, in thick fog. There were 2,207 passengers on board, but only twenty lifeboats; fifteen hundred people died.

JUNGLES

The jungles of the world are being eroded at the rate of fourteen acres every minute.

The Amazon basin comprises one-twentieth of the land area of the planet, and contains one-fifth of its fresh water sources and one-third of its forests. Through plant photosynthesis, it is thought to produce up to half of the oxygen added to the atmosphere each year. Yet one-quarter of the Amazon jungle was deforested between 1966 and 1975 alone, and the process of clearing the jungle is increasing at the rate of thirty percent a year. The deforestation of the Amazon basin has been described as "environmentally suicidal" and "like getting rid of one of the world's major oceans."

KANGAROOS   KISSING

KANGAROOS

Kangaroos received their name when Captain Cook's crew asked Australian aborigines what those strange creatures hopping about were. They answered, "Kangaroo," which means "What are you saying?"

The smallest kangaroo is the narbalek, which is only 12 inches tall and weighs about 4 pounds. The largest is the red kangaroo, which can grow up to 8 feet 11 inches and weigh 180 pounds.

KISSING

A course on "Social Kissing—Puckering and Protocol," is offered by the Open University of Washington, D.C. Run by Joe-Jeff Goldblatt, it includes instruction on the Air Kiss, the Inhalation Kiss, and the Dart and Dodge Kiss, and offers advice on Fending Off the French Kiss.

Goldblatt's instructions on the Dart and Dodge Kiss for the uninitiated are: "Aim directly for the lips of your partner and, a split second before contact, dart around the cheek to the left or right. This is very difficult to master and can lead to an Ear Kiss if the timing is off. If you've ever been kissed unexpectedly in the ear, you know that's pretty serious."

The longest single kiss on record was between two Brazilians who caused a traffic jam in 1964 when, during a quick embrace in their car, their dental braces became intertwined.

Paul Trevillion and Sadie Nine, world champion kissers, train by cycling two miles every day and by rubbing their lips with sunflower oil and seawater. Paul claims, "Sadie has a pair of sexy lips. Her lower lip is now twice the size it was when we started." In Cleveland in 1975, they established a world record of 20,009 kisses in two hours.

An Australian man who has had no feeling in his lips since he was injured in a car crash was awarded $142,000 by the New South Wales Supreme Court because he cannot kiss.

LAST WORDS LIMB RESTORATION

LAUGHING GAS LLAMAS

LAW LOVE AND

LEECHES ATTRACTION

LIGHTNING

LAST WORDS

"Die?" said Viscount Palmerston on his deathbed in 1865. "Die, my dear doctor? That's the last thing I shall do!" And he did.

"We are all going to heaven," said the painter Thomas Gainsborough on a similar occasion, adding with anticipation, "and Vandyke is of the company."

From Julius Caesar's "Et tu, Brute?" to William Turner's triumphant cry, "The sun is God!" and Citizen Kane's single enigmatic word, "Rosebud," there is something about Famous Last Words. Maybe it's the captive audience, or the God-given opportunity for showing off, or simply because they are so final, but most famous people think a good one-liner is expected of them when the time comes.

Sometimes the actual words are in doubt. Did Lord Nelson really say to Hardy, captain of the *Victory*, "Kiss me, Hardy," or was it "Kismet, Hardy?" It doesn't matter. One can even forgive the examples that are too neat to be convincing. Were Queen Elizabeth I's last words really, "All my possessions for a moment of time?" Did King George V actually ask, "How is the Empire?" Maybe, maybe not. But every so often a story comes down to us that has the ring of truth about it. It is on record, for instance, that Henry V roused himself from his final delirium to hear the monks chanting, "Build yet the walls of Jerusalem," and in his confused state the dying king thought the words were addressed to him. "Good Lord," he stammered, "Thou knowest that mine intent hath been to re-edify the walls of Jerusalem—and yet it is, if I might live."

Royalty tend to die rather publicly and, according to the historian Macaulay, Charles II apologized to those around him for spending an unconscionable amount of time dying, and hoped they would excuse him. In the end, still faithful to his mistress Nell Gwyn, his last words were, "Let not poor Nelly starve." As thoughtful, believable, and famous an exit line as one could want.

When there is a conflict of evidence, the unofficial account is usually the better one. In the official version, the last words of the eighteenth-century politician, William

Pitt, are supposed to have been, "My country, O my country." But who would believe *that* in the face of the unauthorized, and far more likely, version in which he rallied at the last moment, sat up, and said, "I think I could eat one of Bellamy's pork pies."

Authors have a natural advantage with the well-turned phrase. "God will pardon me," said Heinrich Heine confidently, "it's his trade." "Turn up the lights," said O. Henry (William Sydney Porter), "I don't want to go home in the dark." Dr. Samuel Johnson, on the other hand, went out on an almost conversational note. According to Boswell he turned to a Miss Morris, who had come to visit him from next door, and simply said, "God bless you, my dear," before dying.

Johnson himself once remarked, "Depend upon it sir, when a man knows he is to be hanged in a fortnight, it concentrates the mind wonderfully." The traditional "speech from the scaffold" certainly brings out the best and worst in people. King Charles I made an interminable political speech, while Louis XVI took a more dramatic line. "Fils de Saint Louis, montes au ciel" ("Son of Saint Louis, mount up to heaven"), he said, climbing the steps to the guillotine. But the prize for ultimate cool goes to Sir Walter Raleigh. "So the heart be right," he joked with the headsman, "it is no matter which way the head lies."

According to Jean de la Fontaine: "Death never takes a wise man by surprise." But to be sure that the press gets it right, the wise man writes his epitaph well in advance. "When I am dead," wrote Hilaire Belloc, "let it be said, 'His sins were scarlet but his books were read.'" Dorothy Parker's chosen epitaph was sharper and shorter: "Excuse my dust." Keats, with a poet's eye for an image, wanted his epitaph to be, "Here lies one whose name is writ in water," but in reality the last words he spoke were simpler and infinitely more touching. Coughing his lungs up, in a room overlooking the Piazza d'Espania in Rome, he called to the friend who was nursing him, "Severn . . . I . . . lift me up . . . I am dying . . . I shall die easy . . . don't be frightened . . . be firm, and thank God it has come."

The shortest and pithiest of Famous Last Words were those of Queen Victoria's son, Edward VII, though for obvious reasons they remain apocryphal. Toward the end of his life, the King suffered a number of illnesses and had made a habit of convalescing at the town of Bognor (which changed its name to Bognor Regis, with royal permission). When his final illness came, his doctors were anxious to reassure him. "Your Majesty's condition is much improved," said one of them. "We have every hope," said another, "that Your Majesty will soon be well enough to visit Bognor again."

"Bugger Bognor," said the monarch, and died.

Dutch Schultz, shot down by rival mobsters anxious to stop him from assassinating the gang-busting D.A. Thomas Dewey in 1935, whispered on his deathbed: "Mother is the best bet . . . and don't let Satan draw you too fast."

LAUGHING GAS

Over a century ago, the following advertisement was circulated in Hartford, Connecticut:

> "A grand exhibition of the effects produced by inhaling Nitrous Oxide, Exhilarating or Laughing Gas, will be given at Union Hall this (Tuesday) evening, December 10, 1844.
>
> Forty gallons of Gas will be prepared and administered to all in the audience who desire to inhale. Twelve Young Men have volunteered to inhale the Gas to commence the entertainment.
>
> Eight Strong Men are engaged to occupy the front seats to protect those under the influence of the Gas from injuring themselves or others. This course is adopted that no apprehension or danger may be entertained. Probably no one will attempt to fight.
>
> The effect of the Gas is to make those who inhale it either Laugh, Sing, Dance, Speak or Fight and so forth, according to the leading trait of their character.

They seem to retain consciousness enough not to say or do that which they would have occasion to regret.

NB—The Gas will be administered only to gentlemen of the first respectability. The object is to make the entertainment in every respect, a genteel affair."

LAW

An eighty-two-year-old U.S. judge was forcibly retired in 1977 after he kept constantly falling asleep on duty (earning himself the nickname "Dozey" in legal circles), and once wore a Shirley Temple wig in court.

A restaurant in Britain was charged with an offense under the 1955 Food and Drugs Act after a customer asked a waiter for a glass of lemonade and was served with caustic soda. The owners appealed their conviction on the grounds that lemonade was not food, but the appeal was dismissed.

A thirty-four-year-old Spokane man filed a $600,000 lawsuit after he was blinded in one eye by a plastic cork shot out of a champagne bottle.

A twenty-nine-year-old woman filed a $20,000 damage suit against the Boston Zoological Society claiming that after a cockatoo had pecked her nose she was left with permanent scarring.

The longest-running court case in recorded history was in ancient Egypt. Around 1350 B.C., members of a shopmaster's family called Neshi began a series of court squabbles over some fifty acres of Nile Valley land, which went on for a century. The whole case was recorded in hieroglyphics, but the panel recording the verdict was missing. After a long search, an archaeologist discovered it, to find that the Neshis had finally won out.

In Washington, D.C., there is a lawyer for every fifty-two people.

Of the thirty-seven articles in the Magna Carta, all but ten have been repealed.

Among the archaic laws only recently repealed in Britain are the Statute of Winchester, which banned fairs being held in graveyards, and a 1605 act that prevented any relatives of Guy Fawkes from holding property.

In Zanzibar (now part of Tanzania), it used to be a capital offense for anyone without a medical qualification to remove tonsils. The death penalty is still mandatory there for clove smugglers.

In one of the more unusual sections of the British Vagrancy Act is an offense listed under Nuisances: "Showing and keeping a booth on Epsom Downs (a racetrack) for an indecent performance to anyone desirous of seeing it."

In Toledo, Spain, a town with very narrow streets, you can be fined 50¢ on the spot for walking more than two abreast.

In 1977, the government-owned railroad system in Italy filed suit against a dead man. Lorenzo Castelli, the suit claimed, held up three trains for up to twenty-nine minutes by "crossing tracks incautiously and being hit by a train."

In 1972, a California assemblyman introduced a bill that would exempt motorists who have lost both hands from paying parking meter fees.

Twenty-four-year-old Tom Hansen of Boulder, Colorado, filed suit against his parents, charging "psychological malparenting" and claiming $350,000 in damages. The Hansen case appears to be the first ever filed by a child seeking damages directly from his parents. Says Hansen: "I realize that it's kind of sacrilegious to sue your parents, kind of like stepping on Mommy's apple pie." Hansen, who has been in and out of mental institutions for several years, says he chose the suit as an alternative to his desire to kill his father.

A $100,000 damage suit was filed in Milwaukee against a robbery victim by the robber, who claimed his victim used excessive force to prevent the crime. Earl Kilgore, the robber, attempted to steal money from William Piotrowski, a service station attendant, at knifepoint. Piotrowski, who at the time of the incident had been robbed at least twenty times before, described the suit as "the most stupid thing I ever heard of." He claimed, "I don't shoot at every customer that comes in. Just those who stick knives in my ribs and rob me."

LEECHES

Leeches are still used in many countries for the purpose of bloodletting. They are even used in America and Britain, in cases where doctors prefer not to make an incision.

The leech is a sluglike creature that can stretch from its normal one-inch length up to five inches when it swims or crawls. It usually lives in water and can survive for twelve months without food. It sucks out blood after sinking its jaws into the victim.

The best way to remove a leech is to put it in salt water, though heroes in Hollywood war films casually burn the beasts off with lighted cigarettes.

Leeches were, at one time, so common as a medical tool that they gave their name to doctors, who were widely known as "leeches" both in the literal sense of being bloodletters and the metaphorical sense of sucking the patient dry of money.

LIGHTNING

Lightning travels at twenty thousand miles a second, can generate a temperature of 27,000 degrees Fahrenheit, and strikes somewhere on Earth about six thousand times every minute. Lightning manufactures about one hundred million tons of nitrogen out of the air each year. A powerful lightning bolt has enough energy to lift a large ocean liner six feet into the air.

A stroke of "fossilized lightning" two hundred million years old was discovered in a sandstone formation in the Navajo Indian Reservation in Arizona. Geologist Michael Purucker identified the fossil because the local magnetic field strength around the discharge is strong enough to remagnetize grains of magnetic minerals in rock samples lying near the lightning's path.

The most powerful lightning stroke recorded in the United States hit the Cathedral of Learning of the University of Pittsburgh on July 31, 1947, discharging 345,000 amps—sufficient current to light 600,000 sixty-watt light-bulbs for the thirty-five millionths of a second of the flash.

A dramatic report of ball lightning came from a house-wife in the Midlands area of England on August 8, 1975. The witness was in her kitchen in Smethwick when, during a vigorous thunderstorm, a sphere of light about ten centimeters in diameter, surrounded by a bright purple-to-blue halo, appeared over the stove. She claimed: "The ball seemed to hit me below the belt, as it were, and I automatically brushed it away from me and it just disappeared. Where I brushed it away there appeared a redness and swelling on my left hand. It seemed as if my gold wedding ring was burned into my finger." The ball vanished with a bang.

Lightning has hit the Empire State Building as often as twelve times in twenty minutes and as frequently as five hundred times in a year.

A scientist at the Stanford Research Institute has estimated that there is a million-to-one chance against a lightning flash striking a picnic held on a quarter-acre area in North Dakota between 3:00 and 4:00 P.M. on Independence Day.

LIMB RESTORATION

The first successful reattachment of a completely severed hand was performed in 1963 by Dr. Chen Chung-Wei in Shanghai, China.

When Mr. Kazumi Kimata, thirty-one, had his arm severed below the elbow in an industrial accident near Nagoya, Japan, doctors told him they couldn't rejoin it. So he took it home, put it in a plastic bag, prayed over it, and buried it in his garden. Six hours later, however, another surgeon offered to try to graft the arm back on, so Mr. Kimata disinterred his arm, took it to the hospital, and had a twelve-hour operation. His arm is now working fine.

Las Vegas doctors sewed back the hand of a twenty-one-year-old woman who had chopped it off with a machete after "sinning against God." She arrived at the hospital quoting the Book of Matthew: "Wherefore if thy hand or thy foot offend thee, cut them off and cast them from thee."

The operation for sewing back a severed penis is extremely difficult and rare. It has so far been carried out on four recorded occasions: twice in 1976, at the Nare Medical University, Japan; once at Boston General Hospital in August, 1977; and most recently, at Emory University Hospital, Atlanta, on October 9, 1977. This last case concerned Milton Cronheim, twenty, who was shortened by James Crompton, twenty-four, to prevent the use of the organ on his wife. Crompton assaulted Cronheim at his apartment at Clemson, South Carolina, while a teenaged relative held a gun on Cronheim's roommate. The victim was held by the neck until unconscious, then he was tied up and his penis was cut off with a knife. The severed penis was reimplanted by Atlanta surgeons using new micro-techniques in an operation lasting seven hours. Three months later the doctors announced that Cronheim "now has full and satisfactory functions."

LLAMAS

Llamas have notoriously bad breath and can wiggle their ears one at a time or together. They can carry a load of ninety pounds for about thirty miles a day at extreme altitudes.

LOVE AND ATTRACTION

The first International Conference on Love and Attraction was held in 1977, and attracted two hundred psychologists and sociologists from all over the world. Several speakers announced that romantic love was dying out, superseded by sexual permissiveness. "Love" was not a word widely used at the conference, however; most people preferred to talk of "amorance," which was defined by one delegate as "the cognitive-affective state characterized by intrusive and obsessive fantasizing concerning reciprocity of amorant feeling by the object of the amorance, or OA." Which means to say you're in love when you get all emotional about someone you're in love with.

MAGIC AND MAGICIANS

The Supreme Magic Company of Bideford, Devon, England, sells the Sacrificial Cremation Outfit, which comes complete with collapsible table, altar, and prayer mat. The outfit enables you, for only $122, to set fire to your friend's head.

Kar-Mi, whose real name was Joseph B. Hallworth, toured the United States with a fifteen-minute act in the early 1900s. Among his tricks was one where he "Swallows a Loaded Gun Barrel . . . and Shoots a Cracker from a Man's Head." It is said that he died of stomach cancer as a result of performing this trick too often.

John Nevil Maskelyne, Britain's most famous nineteenth-century magician, was the descendant of the Reverend John Nevil Maskelyne (b. 1732), who was Astronomer Royal for forty-three years and for whom the moon crater Maskelyne was named.

Maskelyne is credited with the invention of the matinee for dramatic performances; also the coin lock (as used in pay toilets), the box-office automatic ticket dispenser, a keyboard typewriter, and a cash register.

He built many automatons, including his famous "Psycho," which played whist and is now preserved at the London Museum in Kensington Palace. His "Zach the Hermit" show, presented at the Egyptian Hall, London, on February 17, 1879, featured a winking moon, an automatic talking parrot, a writhing mechanical snake, an animated table, and a dancing walking stick.

In the 1840s, magician Robert-Houdin had a mechanical tree that produced oranges in which a borrowed handkerchief appeared. Butterflies unfolded the handkerchief in midair.

Alexander Herrmann, America's leading magician from 1870 to 1890, pulled a roll of bills from the beard of the mayor of New York City, who had just performed his wedding ceremony. He also once pulled a handful of cigars from the whiskers of President Ulysses S. Grant. Herrmann owned a private railway car costing $40,000, which had once belonged to Lillie Langtry.

In 1953, the magician John Mulholland was paid $3,000 to write a manual for CIA agents on sleight of hand, which they could then use to administer drugs surreptitiously.

MALE GENITALIA

An academic study by a New Zealand scientist into the genitalia of Greek and Roman statues revealed that in 600 B.C. all testicles were created equal, but by 480 B.C. the pattern had changed: the right testicle was always higher, the left one always larger.

The auction catalogue identified it as a "small dried-up object, genteelly described as a mummified tendon taken from Napoleon's body during the postmortem." It was put up for auction in London in 1969 by an American named Bruce Gimelson, age twenty-seven, but the highest price offered for the imperial relic was $38,000, well below the reserve price. A disappointed Mr. Gimelson said afterward, "You can't put a value on it, it's unique," and added that he hoped to sell it to the French government. It was Napoleon's penis.

MARIJUANA

Two large baskets of cannabis sativa some twenty-two hundred years old were discovered on board the remains of a Carthaginian warship that had gone down off the coast of Sicily during the First Punic War with Rome. Protected by anaerobic conditions, it was still potent.

When Malcolm X was a teenage reefer man in Harlem, he was known as Detroit Red.

In the United States in 1941, when the paranoid anti-marijuana campaign was at its height, magazines outdid themselves in an attempt to convey the true horror of the noxious weed to their readers. One such report, entitled *America's Most Dangerous Drug*, tells of a "marijuana jag party" in Grand Forks, North Dakota. Here white women, some with bags over their heads to "inhale all the smoke from the reefer," danced wildly with black men in zippy suits. The photo caption read: "Leaping high, these two vipers break into rhythmic hand-clapping to the torrid tunes of the automatic phonograph or joy-box."

The huge research effort into marijuana, fueled by public paranoia, now means we know more about the herb than we do about penicillin.

In 1795, Archibald Cochrane, ninth Earl of Dundonald, suggested that hemp or marijuana plants be cultivated on the peat mosses of Scotland as a source of oil. "Were hemp cultivated on an extensive scale in this country," he wrote, "the expressed oil from the seeds might be advantageously applied to the manufacture of soap, of a superior quality to that which is now made from tallow." The idea was never carried out.

MARRIAGE

Two Italian diving enthusiasts, Arturo Santora and Barbara Durante, were married on the seabed in San Frutuosos Bay, near Geneva. The priest and all the witnesses were in full diving gear, and the bride carried a bouquet of coral.

The patron saint of marriage is Sao Goncalo, a thirteenth-century Benedictine monk, and every year a festival is held in his honor at Amarante, northern Portugal. The traditional food served is phallic-shaped egg-yolk pastries. Pilgrims travel to his tomb and rub their bodies against his crypt, hoping a husband or wife will come with the scratches.

An eighty-eight-year-old Iranian who had been married 168 times attributed his sexual prowess to eating two pounds of uncooked onions every day.

A 117-year-old man, Lebai Omar Bin Datuk Panghima, was fined eighty dollars in Malaysia for living with his forty-year-old lover without marrying her, a violation of Moslem law. They later married.

The Caxton Hall registry office in London, which closed in November, 1977, was the scene of the marriages of Elizabeth Taylor, Roger Moore, and Peter Sellers. Among the stranger marriages performed there was one wedding where the bride wanted her two dogs as witnesses, and a dancer who wanted to be married with her snake twined around her neck.

The traditional view of Puritan morality is somewhat belied by the custom of "bundling," which was widely practiced in the seventeenth century by diehard Protestants in northern Europe and New England.

Bundling involved a courting or betrothed couple spending the night together in the girl's bedroom in a carefully restricted anticipation of the intimacies of marriage. A kind of formalized version of necking in automobiles, the couple had to keep their clothes on, were separated by layers of bedding, and were expected to behave with "reasonable" propriety.

MASS ANIMAL ATTACKS

Although they are a favorite theme of science fiction, mass attacks by animals on human beings are comparatively rare events—but they do happen. Two horrifying examples occurred within a few months of each other in 1945, during the closing stages of World War II.

When the U.S. cruiser *Indianapolis* was torpedoed by a Japanese submarine in the Pacific, hundreds of sailors, many of them injured, found themselves in shark-infested waters. The blood attracted frenzied packs of the creatures, and before they could be rescued, two-thirds of the entire crew had been torn to pieces.

The other episode occurred in the same war zone at roughly the same time, on Ramree Island off the coast of Burma. On the night of February 19, 1945, a large number of retreating Japanese soldiers took refuge from the encircling British troops by wading waist-deep into a brackish island swamp. Bruce Wright, a naturalist, was there at the time and described what happened:

"The din of the barrage had caused all the crocodiles within miles to slide into the water and lie with only their eyes above, watchfully alert. When it subsided, the ebbing tide brought to them more strongly and in greater volume than they had ever known it before, the scent and taste that aroused them as nothing else—the smell of blood. Silently each snout turned into the current and the great tails began to weave from side to side . . ."

It was one of the largest recorded massacres of its kind. After the crocodiles moved in at dusk, only twenty out of the one thousand men survived.

MASS HYSTERIA

The male inhabitants of certain parts of Malaya and Thailand occasionally experience the mass conviction that their penises are shrinking. The rumor usually starts with some specific cause—in the 1976 outbreak, for instance, it was said that Thai oranges were causing the condition—and spreads like wildfire. The men become obsessed with the size of their sexual organs and are unable to pay attention to anything else.

Fits of uncontrollable laughter periodically spread like an epidemic among adolescent girls in Tanzania. In Zanzibar in 1977, eighteen girls were hospitalized with the condition and many schools had to be temporarily closed.

One of the most notorious modern cases of mass hysteria occurred in 1955, in London, when nearly three hundred members of the medical, nursing, and ancillary staff at the Royal Free Hospital succumbed to a disease that bore all the symptoms of polio. Tests, however, showed that they did not have polio at all, and all of them recovered. Even more strange was the fact that almost none of the patients at the hospital were affected.

MEASUREMENT

The standard kilogram weight, against which all others in the world are measured, is known as "K," and is kept inside three glass domes in an underground chamber near Paris. It has not been touched for thirty years because, as the vice-director of the International Bureau of Weights and Measures explains: "Every use of the kilogram inevitably disturbs its weight in some manner, however careful we are. Even if we could guard against superficial abrasions—and a scratch that removes one ten-millionth of it would be dishearteningly noticeable—there is always the problem of dust accumulation. For example, the British national copy of the kilogram is used quite frequently, and although stored most carefully, it has gained substantial weight in the past half-century due to London's gritty air." K is the only standard that hasn't been replaced by an atomic definition, because serious technical problems are involved and attempts to date have been less accurate than the solid K.

Santoro Sanctorius, founder of the science of metabolism, spent much of his time, over a thirty-year period, sitting on a weighing device to calculate variations in his body weight before and after eating, drinking, sleeping, exercise, and so on. He carefully weighed all the food and drink he ingested as well as the excreta that he passed, and was able to make exact measurements of the weight he lost due to water evaporation.

MERMAIDS AND MERMEN

Myths and sightings of mermaids are many and various. Henry Hudson, the famous explorer, sighted several near Novaya Zemlya, in the Arctic Ocean north of Russia. He described one of them as being "as big as one of us, her skin very white and long hair hanging down behind, of color black. In her going down we saw her tail which was like the tail of a porpoise, speckled like a mackerel . . . (but) from the navel upward, her back and breasts were like a woman's."

The mermaid myth may have been based on sightings of the manatee or sea cow, the female of which has breasts placed as on a woman's body, suckles her young, and even cries when excited.

About 1825, the Reverend Robert Hawker, an English clergyman and practical joker, decided to test the power of the mermaid myth. He swam out to an offshore rock near Bude in Cornwall, and sat there naked to the waist, with an oilskin "tail" about his legs and his hair entwined with seaweed, preening himself in a mirror. When the moon rose, he began to sing an eerie song. For several nights running, large, awestruck crowds gathered on the beach to observe the remarkable phenomenon, until Hawker, wearied of the jest, burst into the lyrics of *God Save the King*, and plunged into the sea.

In 1956, a confidence trickster entered a bank in Accra, the capital of Ghana, dressed as a mermaid. He told the astonished bank cashier to give him $1,110 and he would immediately double it. The cashier did so, and the man/mermaid walked out with the money.

METEORITES

Only one person is known to have been hit by a meteorite. On November 30, 1954, Mrs. E. Hodges of Aylacauga,

Alabama, was sitting at home having lunch when a nine-pound meteorite crashed through her roof and hit her in the upper thigh. She was not seriously hurt.

Possibly the largest meteorite fall ever witnessed by man flashed across the skies over China around 3:00 P.M. on March 8, 1976. As it entered the atmosphere and plunged four hundred kilometers, it burned brighter than the full moon. The rock broke into several large pieces that landed in the province of Kirun; the largest chunk fell sixty-five meters from the nearest house and thirty meters from six commune members. Witnesses reported that they heard what sounded like a sonic boom, and a grayish mass "like a huge jar" hit the ground with "an appalling roar." The space rock drilled its way six meters into the ground, creating an elliptical crater some two meters across. A dense cloud of yellow smoke and dust rose from the crater to a height of fifty meters, forming a small mushroom cloud. The specimen, once disinterred, was about one cubic meter in volume and weighed 1,170 kilograms (2,586 pounds). It is estimated that the meteorite, the largest known, hit the Earth at some three hundred meters per second.

In the excavation of a Mexican temple, a meteorite was found wrapped in mummy clothes.

MINIATURES

When India gave the Soviet Union a present of a needle with seven elephants carved into it, the Russians called on Armenian micro-artist Edward Kazarian to devise a suitable present in return. He polished a hair with diamond dust, hollowed it out, and inserted three hundred carved elephants inside it.

A Ukrainian craftsman, using a high-powered microscope, sewed together the strands of a spider's web to make a twelve-page book.

In the nineteenth century, miniature writing was very popular and competition was keen. A certain Mr. Goldberg produced a legible image of a page with fifty lines of print, each line being less than a tenth of a millimeter in height. This meant it would take 87,500 such pages to fill a square inch, a figure equivalent to fifty Bibles. In fact, "Bibles per square inch" became a standard measuring device of the time.

MODELING

The world's first modeling agency was founded by John Robert Powers in New York in the 1920s, after he overheard some businessmen saying that they needed some attractive people to pose for a magazine advertisement. Among the famous people who once worked as Powers's models were Constance Bennett, Barbara Stanwyck, Tyrone Power, Fredric March, and Henry Fonda.

MONEY

The oldest bank notes are the "flying money" or convenient money, first issued in China in 2697 B.C. Printed in blue ink on paper made from the fiber of the mulberry tree, they bore the legend: "Produce all you can; spend with economy."

Teeth currency is common in the South Pacific and among native Americans. On Manam Island in New Guinea, for instance, the women wear monetary necklaces made of dogs' canine teeth; five teeth form one unit of currency worth about ten cents. In the Solomon Islands, ten dolphin teeth are worth about the same, and it takes a phenomenal number to purchase a wife. In Fiji, they use strings of the lower jawbones of fruit bats. In America, the Shoshone and Bannock tribes of Idaho and Montana value the canine teeth of elks at about twenty-five cents each, but use them only in transactions with each other—never with whites.

In 1977, John Shepphard, a British boardinghouse owner, paid a rates bill covering local government costs on a monster check measuring seven feet six inches long by three feet wide.

The same year, a Californian woman paid a tax bill with a check signed on rose-colored panties, and a taxpayer in Salt Lake City paid a garbage bill on a toilet paper check.

There are an estimated ten thousand different credit cards issued in the United States.

The biggest pawnshop in the world is Rome's Monte di Pieta (Mountain of Mercy). In 1976, Romans made 37.7 billion lire (forty-three million dollars) worth of transactions involving 344,325 articles there; an estimated fifty thousand women pawn their furs every summer. Monte di Pieta was founded in 1539 by Giovanni Calvo, a Franciscan monk, who had been ordered by Pope Paul III to find a way to combat the usury of the moneylenders, who were charging people an eighty-six percent interest rate.

An archivist has discovered that during the War of 1812, New York lent Washington one million dollars to build fortifications—and the debt was never repaid. It has been calculated that, with compound interest, the Federal government now owes New York $11,200 million.

In 1976, country-and-western singer Johnny Paycheck declared bankruptcy.

A French company, which planned to haul icebergs to Saudi Arabia, had to go into voluntary liquidation.

The odds against a British girl marrying a millionaire are twenty-five thousand to one. In America, the odds shorten to 2,900 to one.

Stephen Girard, America's first millionaire, was fond of saying, "When death comes for me, he will find me busy."

A production of the comic opera *The Flying Dutchman* (not the opera by Wagner), performed in New York on May 5, 1903, featured the daughters of fifteen millionaires in the chorus.

Grand Cayman Island, a popular tax haven in the Caribbean, has ninety-five banks and more telex cables per capita than any other spot on Earth.

In the United Kingdom, the top one percent of the population (some 340,000 individuals) owns twenty-three percent of the country's total personal wealth. Their average net worth is $233,100. In the United States, the top one percent owns 25.9 percent of the wealth, according to the U.S. government publication, "Data on the Distribution of Wealth.'

A girl who used her pet parakeet as a reference to open a bank account was sent to a reformatory for cashing a worthless check.

MONSTERS

In *Fabulous Beasts and Demons* by Heinz Mode, the following creatures are listed:

A *Bishop-Fish*, which, with an attendant scaly *Water-Monk*, was a guest at the court of the King of Poland in 1546, until he indicated by signs that he wanted to return to the sea.

Sciapods, who have just one vast foot, which they use to shade themselves from the heat of the sun.

The *Psezpolnica*, a Wendish [Slavic German] horse-footed witch who beheads any passerby who cannot talk for one hour about flax.

The *Burmese Water-Elephant*, as small as a mouse but of enormous strength, which feeds on the brains of normal-sized elephants.

The *Icelandic Skoffin*, a cross between a tomcat and a vixen, whose gaze is fatal.

Cherufels, gigantic Andean creatures that eat girls and live in volcanoes.

THE MOST-TRAVELED CORPSE

The most-traveled corpse in the world is that of Eva Peron, vivacious cult figure and former dictatress of Argentina. When she died of cancer on July 26, 1952, her body was elaborately embalmed and laid in state. Three years later, a military coup overthrew her husband and her body was mysteriously smuggled out of the country and buried in a suburb of Milan, Italy.

Then, in 1971, Eva was dug up and sent to be with her husband in Madrid, where she stayed for three years. Señor Peron returned to power and died in office on July 1, 1976, and on the orders of his second wife, Eva's remains were finally flown home on a chartered airline to be buried beside him in the family crypt.

An ironic twist to the story is that the body of President Pedro Aramburu, the man responsible for having Eva's remains sent out of the country, was stolen, only to be returned when Eva's corpse was back on Argentinian soil.

MOUNTAINS AND MOUNTAINEERING

There is a seven-year waiting list to climb Mt. Everest. Since May 29, 1953, when Hillary and Tenzing were the first to reach its summit, sixty-three men and two women have duplicated their feat.

It was George Leigh Mallory, one of the first men to die trying to climb Mt. Everest, who, when asked why he wanted to scale the peak, replied, "Because it's there."

The world's second highest mountain, K2, was originally named after Henry Haversham Godwin-Austen, the man who discovered it in 1856, during the British India Survey—but his name refused to stick.

In 1974, a West German expedition scaled Annapurna Four by mistake, instead of Annapurna Two. The Nepalese government banned them from having another try on the right mountain.

In 1975, a British expedition made mountaineering history by planning their climb of the 25,800-foot Nuptse Peak using a computer to do critical path analysis.

Five blind boys climbed the 16,350-foot Lenana Peak of Mt. Kenya in just four days in 1977, accompanied by three teachers and nine porters. (Incidentally, the U.S. National Park Service has set up a study group to teach blind people the techniques of rock climbing.)

In 1978, thirty-seven-year-old Yukihiro Isa, who is paralyzed from the waist down, climbed 12,388-foot Mount Fuji in five days—in a one-horsepower wheelchair, accompanied by nurses and technicians.

Climber Wolfgang Gorter was so angry that Germany's highest mountain, Zugspitze, was only 2,964 meters high, that he built a concrete tower on top to make it a 3,000-meter mountain.

Aconcagua, in Argentina, the forty-third highest mountain in the world, has the reputation of being a killer, surrounded as it is by vicious, changeable weather. At least one hundred people have died attempting to climb it, and many of them now lie buried in a special "cemetery of the defeated" at the foot of the mountain. Its strange microclimate causes hallucinations; one experienced climber claimed he saw horses dancing on the summit.

MUSICAL INSTRUMENTS

The ultimate electronic one-man band is an instrument called the Symphonic Theater Console, which is played like an organ and can produce the sounds of: the golden harp, percussion with eight voices, fifteen upper-keyboard voices, flute chorus, orchestral symphonizer with sixteen voices, guitar or ukulele strum, piano or harpsichord, arpeggio, boogie-woogie bass, symphonic strings, four manual rhythm voices, bass, string bass, or guitar bass.

NAIL BITING

More than fifteen percent of Americans secretly bite their toenails, according to a psychologist at Brigham Young University.

NAMES

Aubrey Russell-Scarr changed his name to Aubrey Mersey Thompson in order to inherit the $1.1 million estate of his spinster cousin, who made it a condition of her will.

David M. Shirk, a self-employed electrician in California, applied to change his name to Garrett Shandler, claiming that his original moniker damaged his business.

Michael Dengler, a former social studies teacher, tried to change his name to 1069 because, he said, "The number symbolized his interrelationship with society and reflected his personal and philosophical identity." The judge ruled against him, however, claiming that a number "is totalitarian and an offense to human dignity."

An estimated six million South Koreans—about one-sixth of the population—are named Kim, all of whom trace their common ancestry back to King Kim Su Ro, who, legend has it, was born from a golden egg and grew to adulthood in seven years.

A retired U.S. Army paratrooper enjoyed parachuting so much that he called his children Ripcord and Canopy.

A report from the official Russian birth registry in Moscow lists such names as Electrification, Combine, and Hydrostation, also twins named Anarchy and Utopia, and a man named Melsor, an acronym for Marx-Engels-Lenin-Stalin-October-Revolution.

Ever since the Biafran War, the Nigerian government has done everything in its power to unite the many diverse tribes of the country. When it came to naming the ships of the Nigerian navy, a number of different tribal languages were used—with the absurd result that Nigeria is now the only naval power to have twenty warships whose names, when translated, all mean hippopotamus.

Adding your name to the language is a good way to go down in history—even if no one remembers exactly who you were. Take flowers for instance: dahlias, magnolias, and poinsettias are all named after people, U.S. Secretary of War Poinsett among them. Clothes, from leotards to bloomers, have frequently picked up their owners' monikers. Nicotine was the first Frenchman who turned on to tobacco, and sideburns were originally the whiskers of General Ambrose Everett Burnside of the Army of the Potomac. Georg Ohm, the German physicist, had it both ways—as the unit of electrical resistance and (backwards) as mho, the name Kelvin gave to the unit of conductivity.

You have to be famous at the time, of course, though if you are *too* famous, the process is liable to get out of hand. Apart from being commemorated by numerous pieces of geography, the Duke of Wellington lived on as boots, fir trees, and a World War II bomber of geodetic design, none of which he had anything to do with. You also have to watch your behavior, as only bad habits tend to get recorded in this way, and being remembered through such words as lynching, quisling, chauvinism, boycott, and hooligan is not the most flattering form of immortality. But what a way to go—or rather stay.

NECKTIES

The British police have taken to recording their exploits with specially designed neckties. The tie that commemorates the armed attempt to kidnap Princess Anne and her husband, Mark Phillips, outside Buckingham Palace a few years ago has the insignia of a golden crown, a golden ball (the attacker's name was Ball), the letters A and M, and the registration number of the royal car, AGN 1. Regular police units are also adopting ties; the Obscene Publications Squad has a piece of blue paper being cut by scissors, and the bomb squad has a bell, book, and candle representing alarm-clock fuses, parcel bombs, and incendiary devices respectively. But the most imaginative (and tasteless) design comes from Scotland Yard's intelligence unit dealing with drugs and illegal immigration. The emblem is an eagle with a broken wing clutching a hypodermic needle. The needle represents drugs, and the bird (take a deep breath) is an "ill eagle."

NEW LANGUAGES

These are some of the new languages that have appeared in the last few centuries. They tend to be international codes that come into being when the existing language of a culture is inadequate to express new ideas.

Esperanto is an auxiliary international language devised in Poland in 1887 by Dr. Zamenhof, whose pseudonym, *Esperantist*, means "the hoping one." Esperantists claim that if adopted by the U.N., the new language would save nearly one million dollars a year in translators' salaries and equipment.

Volapük, the first international language, was invented in 1880 by an Austrian priest.

Basic English is a simplified language of 850 words developed by C. K. Ogden in the 1930s. "Basic" is an acronym of British American Scientific International Commercials. This is how it translates the *Lord's Prayer*:

Father of all up in the sky
You get our deepest respect
We hope our nation with you
as king for ruler will come
down to us.
We hope you have your way
in the place we live as on high
Give us food for now, and

overlook wrongdoing as we
overlook wrongdoing by persons to us.
Please guide us from courses of
desire, and keep us from badness.

Pidgin English has been in use for about four hundred years. It was originally developed as a sort of colonialist Esperanto in South America and Africa, and is still widely spoken in West Africa and New Guinea. The word "pidgin" is thought to derive from the Pidian tribe in South America.

When the Solomon Islands in the Pacific became independent after eighty-five years of British rule, the Duke of Gloucester, representing the Queen, read the following message:

"Tede wanfala big dei, hemi kam nao. Kantri blong yufala hem grou ap an kwin hemi wenten evri samting blong yufala, i kam ap gudfala long olgeta ias. Babae i kam."

In English: "Today is a big day. Your country has grown up and the Queen wants to see that everything you have and do may turn out well in the years to come."

Incidentally, the new governor general, Baddeley Devesi, is also the Solomons' snooker champion.

Science may not sound like a new language, but it is. There is no other word for an exclusive vocabulary of over 300,000 words, mostly invented in our lifetime, understood and used by people around the world in the same way that Latin was used in the Middle Ages, with its own unique syntax (math and algebra) and describing subjects (like nuclear physics) for which there are no words in other languages. What is more, unlike other languages, which tend to replace one word with another, the scientific language is growing.

NEWSPAPERS

One of the smallest newspapers ever produced was the one-and-a-half-inch by two-inch copy of the London *Times* issued in 1924 to commemorate the Queen's Doll House at the Empire Exhibition.

The following are names of newspapers published in the Wild West in the nineteenth century:

Kansas Prairie Dog, Cheyenne County Rustler, Clark County Clipper, Cash City Cashier, Morganville News and Sunflower, The Saturday Cyclone, The Brick, The Eye, The Allison Breeze and Times, The Head Centre and Daily Morning Sun, The Broad Axe, Grip, Locomotive, Kansas Cowboy, The Ryansville Boomer, Hill City Lively Times, Western Cyclone, Conductor Punch, Cimarron Herald and Kansas Sod House, The Montezuma Chief, Ensign Razzoop, Border Ruffian, The Jayhawker and Palladium, Santa Fe Trail, Comanche Chief and Kiowa Chief, Daily Infant Wonder, The Scout, Gopher, and Winona, The Hatchet, The Fanatic, The Comet, The Boomerang, The Hornet, The Wasp, Astonisher and Paralyzer, Inkslinger's Advertiser, Grisby City Scorcher, Sunday Growler, The Prairie Owl, Springfield Soap Box, The Whim-Wham, Sherman County Dark Horse, The Bazoo, Thomas County Cat, and Grit.

The *International Herald Tribune* of November 23, 1902, reported that a Viennese bank director, assisted by two friends who were lawyers, had decided to publish a newspaper for nervous persons. He claimed: "Catastrophes like that at Martinique, big bank failures, and other events calculated to upset the nerves will be treated in a soothing way so as not to disturb sensitive people."

On December 3, 1961, *The New York Times* published a record edition. Each issue contained 678 pages and the press run was 1,458,558 copies. Manufacturing the pulp for the necessary 4,550 tons of paper required the wood from over 77,000 full-grown trees. Their average age was 70 years, and cutting them left a 360-acre hole in the forest. All this to publish a single edition of a single newspaper in a single city, read in the morning and thrown away in the afternoon.

NOBEL PRIZE

The impetus that made Alfred Nobel set up his foundation is alleged to have been an obituary notice published ten years before his death, which assessed his life in a disparaging manner as having been that of a dynamite manufacturer.

Nobel once wrote of himself: "Alfred Nobel, a miserable half-life, ought to have been choked to death by a philanthropic physician as soon as, with a howl, he entered life."

THE NOGUCHI TELEGRAM

The most compressed, and arguably the most beautiful, expression in any language is E = MC², although the information is implied rather than stated. The problem of actually spelling out Einstein's classic formula was a challenge taken up by R. Buckminster Fuller in one of the most extraordinary telegrams ever sent through the mail.

The famous Japanese sculptor, Isamu Noguchi, had sent Fuller the startling request: "Please wire me rush Einstein's formula and explanation." The question would have stopped any ordinary mortal in his tracks but, undaunted, the guru of modern technology managed to get it all into one telegram. Here it is—an explanation of the Theory of Relativity and its implications in exactly 249 words flat:

EINSTEIN'S FORMULA DETERMINATION INDIVIDUAL SPECIF-
ICS RELATIVITY READS "ENERGY EQUALS MASS TIMES THE SPEED
OF LIGHT SQUARED" SPEED OF LIGHT IDENTICAL SPEED ALL
RADIATION COSMIC GAMMA X ULTRAVIOLET INFRARED RAYS
ETC. ONE HUNDRED EIGHTY THOUSAND MILES PER SECOND
WHICH SQUARED IS TOP OR PERFECT SPEED GIVING SCIENCE A
FINITE VALUE FOR BASIC FACTOR IN MOTION UNIVERSE. SPEED
OF RADIANT ENERGY BEING DIRECTIONAL OUTWARD ALL DIREC-
TIONS EXPANDING WAVE SURFACE DIAMETRIC POLAR SPEED
AWAY FROM SELF IS TWICE SPEED IN ONE DIRECTION AND SPEED
OF VOLUME INCREASE IS SQUARE TO SPEED IN ONE DIRECTION
APPROXIMATELY THIRTY-FIVE BILLION VOLUMETRIC MILES PER
SECOND. FORMULA IS WRITTEN LETTER E FOLLOWED BY EQUA-

TION MARK FOLLOWED BY LETTER M FOLLOWED BY LETTER C
FOLLOWED CLOSELY BY ELEVATED SMALL FIGURE TWO SYMBOL
OF SQUARING. ONLY VARIABLE IN FORMULA IS SPECIFIC MASS
SPEED IS UNIT OF RATE WHICH IS AN INTEGRATED RATIO OF
BOTH TIME AND SPACE AND NO GREATER RATE OF SPEED THAN
THAT PROVIDED BY ITS CAUSE WHICH IS PURE ENERGY LATENT
OR RADIANT IS ATTAINABLE. THE FORMULA THEREFORE PRO-
VIDES A UNIT AND A RATE OF PERFECTION TO WHICH THE REL-
ATIVE IMPERFECTION OR INEFFICIENCY OF ENERGY RELEASE IN
RADIANT OR CONFINED DIRECTION OF ALL TEMPORAL SPACE
PHENOMENA MAY BE COMPARED BY ACTUAL CALCULATION.
SIGNIFICANCE: SPECIFIC QUALITY OF ANIMATES IS CONTROL
WILLFUL OR OTHERWISE OF RATE AND DIRECTION ENERGY
RELEASE AND APPLICATION NOT ONLY TO SELF-MECHANISM
BUT OF FROM-SELF-MACHINE DIVIDED MECHANISMS. RELATIV-
ITY OF ALL ANIMATES AND INANIMATES IS POTENTIAL OF
ESTABLISHMENT THROUGH EINSTEIN FORMULA.

Now do you understand? Good.

THE NORDIC LOOK

Several thousand years ago, a subtle biochemical change
among the population of Scandinavia altered the buildup
of melanin, the chemical responsible for the coloring of
hair, skin, and eyes. The result was the typical "Nordic
look": fair hair, white skin, blue or gray eyes. When the
Norsemen took to ravaging distant lands, they took their
genes with them and the Nordic look spread across northern Europe, and eventually to North America. But a recent
study shows that in France, in the last three hundred years,
the blue-eyed trend is on the wane; dark eyes have now
become the majority.

NUDISTS

One advantage of being a nudist is that you are unlikely
to be chased by bulls. This potentially vital piece of information came to light when a Frenchman got fed up with

members of a nudist colony who took a shortcut across his property to the beach. He bought two dozen ferocious bulls to solve the problem, but the bulls only attacked people wearing clothes and left the nudists alone—apparently regarding them as harmless animals.

A California organization called LIBRE (Living in the Buff Residential Enterprises) specializes in building what it calls "clothing-optional apartments."

NUNS

A nun from Perth, Australia, was unable to accept the $143,989 damages awarded to her for injuries she received in a car crash, because she had taken vows of poverty.

While interviewing for her book *Nuns*, journalist Marcelle Bernstein was picked up outside the Los Angeles Hilton by a member of the Sisters of the Humility of Mary who was wearing curlers, a bikini top and Bermuda shorts, and was driving a white sports car.

A study by American scientist Martha McLintock into all-female institutions in the United States revealed that nuns, like other institutionalized women, menstruate in synchrony, but that cloistered orders menstruated over longer cycles than orders who came into contact with men. She also demonstrated that nuns responded to a male smell by speeding up their menstrual cycles.

OBELISK

The ancient obelisk now standing in New York's Central Park was obtained by William Henry Hulbert, editor of the New York *World*, who asked the Khedive of Egypt, Ismail Pasha, for the monument in 1869, to show his friendship toward America.

When asked which obelisk he would like, Mr. Hulbert reportedly replied, "Forgive the pun, Your Highness, but any old obelisk will do."

OCTOPUSH

Octopush is the official name for underwater hockey. Played eight to a team, it is a game devised in 1954 by divers trying to add an element of fun to their training routines. The object of the game is to propel a four-pound lead disk called a "squid" along the bottom of the pool with a "pusher," into the other team's goal, or "gully."

OLD AGE

Old age is not a sudden phenomenon that strikes at the age of sixty or seventy. The adult body dies a little every day. Most tissues, organs, and physical processes begin to deteriorate when you are in your middle or late twenties, but the degree of deterioration can differ dramatically. The flow of blood to the brain of a seventy-five-year-old is eighty percent of what it was when he was thirty years old. His total brain weight, on the other hand, is only fifty-six percent. His maximum work rate for a short burst has declined to forty percent, and his total number of taste buds is only thirty-six percent of the total number at age thirty. Why the number of taste buds should decline so dramatically with age remains a mystery.

THE OLDEST JIGSAW PUZZLE IN THE WORLD

The oldest jigsaw puzzle in the world was discovered in 1954 when a road was being built near the Great Pyramid of Giza, resting place of the pharaoh Cheops. Under a series of parallel stone blocks, which the centuries had hidden beneath a sand hill, lay a niche cut in the limestone 4,700 years ago. In the niche were found a large number of ropes and reed mats, and 1,224 separate pieces of wood, ranging in length from ten centimeters to twenty-two meters and neatly arranged in thirteen crisscrossing layers. Each piece of wood was marked with chiseled hieroglyphics indicating its position in the puzzle.

The task of putting the puzzle together was given to Egyptian master restorer Ahmed Youssef. It was a long job. He took eighteen months just to remove the wood from the niche, as many of the pieces had partially rotted or bent out of shape and had to be restored. Each was individually photographed, listed, and entered in a filing system under five separate categories.

Youssef took another four years to build the puzzle. There were no nails; the pieces were held together with pegs and ropes. The object, when it finally emerged, was forty-two meters long and portrayed the graceful lines of Cheops' funeral barge, from the papyrus standard in the bow, symbol of southern Egypt, to the lotus standard in the stern, symbol of northern Egypt.

The boat is believed to have transported the corpse of the pharaoh from ancient Memphis, where he ruled about 2,700 B.C., to Giza, where he was mummified and buried.

OLYMPICS

From 1900 to 1920, the Olympic Games contained such sports as cricket, croquet, throwing the javelin with both hands, men's club swinging, underwater swimming, and an obstacle swimming race.

Two teams of pygmies competed in the 1904 Olympics in St. Louis.

The first international dispute of the modern Olympics was in 1908, when the Stockholm police protested that their defeat by the London police in the tug-of-war event was due to their rivals' specially designed shoes.

To the embarrassment of the International Olympic Committee, it was discovered that the idea of transporting the Olympic flame was conceived by Adolf Hitler for the 1936 Summer Olympics in Berlin.

In 1975, Canada's ambassador to Argentina was embarrassed to discover that COJO, the acronym for the Montreal Olympic Games Organizing Committee, was an Argentinian expression roughly meaning "to make love," and that ORTO, the acronym for Olympic Radio and Television Organization, was Argentinian for ass.

There is a world Olympic Games for the Deaf.

ONE IN A MILLION

Mrs. Marva Drew, a fifty-one-year-old housewife from Waterloo, Iowa, typed out every number from one to one million after her son's teacher told him it was impossible to count up to a million. It took her five years and 2,473 sheets of typing paper.

OPIUM

In his book *Opium*, Jean Cocteau claims, "Picasso used to say to me: 'The smell of opium is the least stupid smell in the world. The only smell one can compare with it is that of a circus or a seaport.' " Cocteau adds his own comment: "Opium is the only vegetable substance which communicates the vegetable state to us. Through it we get an idea of that other speed of plants."

The fact that common lettuce contains an opiumlike substance was first discovered by James Johnston, professor of chemistry at the University of Durham in the nineteenth century. In his book *The Chemistry of Common Life* (1854), he wrote:

"The juice of these plants, when collected and dried, has considerable resemblance to opium. If the stem of the common lettuce, when it is coming into flower, be wounded with a knife, a milky juice exudes. In the open air, this juice gradually assumes a brown colour, and dries into a friable mass. The smell of this dried juice is strongly narcotic, recalling that of opium. It has a slightly pungent taste, but, like opium, leaves a permanent bitterness in the mouth. It acts upon the brain after the manner of opium . . . eaten at night, the lettuce causes sleep; eaten during the day it soothes and calms and allays the tendency to nervous irritability."

Legend has it that Buddha, in order to prevent sleep from creeping up on him, cut off his eyelids. Where they fell, there grew an herb which bore a nodding violet flower—the opium poppy.

ORCHIDS

The word "orchid" derives from the Greek *orchis*, meaning "testicles," due to the fact that most Mediterranean orchids have a pair of rounded tubers. In medieval England, orchids were nicknamed "bull's bags."

One of the largest plant families, with 35,000 different species, some orchids produce different perfumes at different times of day. The Moth Orchid, for instance, produces a lily-of-the-valley scent by day, a roselike smell at night. Other orchids smell of bad meat.

The Australian Flying Duck Orchid traps insects for a short time, after tossing them into the center of its flower by using its "lip," shaped like a duck's head.

Bee Orchids have flowers designed like the sex organs of female insects, which exude a strong sexual scent. The insect attempts to mate with the flower—an act called pseudocopulation—and its sex organs are stimulated, but not enough to produce ejaculation. This explains why insects can often be observed biting the petals of the orchids in frustration.

ORIGINS OF WORDS

Chauffeur comes from the French word for medieval bandits, who used to force their luckless victims to run over red-hot coals.

Sarcophagus derives from the Greek for "flesh eater"—so called because of the corrosive effect of early limestone coffins on the bodies interred in them.

A Seattle man has created a new word—*catmatic*—the opposite of dogmatic. It means one who pussyfoots around.

All the following words are derived from Arabic:
Algebra comes from *aljebr*, meaning a reunion of broken parts.
Average comes from *awairy*, the term for damaged goods. Its original usage referred to the amount of a ship's cargo that could be expected to be lost through unavoidable accidents.
Tabby, as in "tabby cat," is named for *attabi*, a cloth with stripes in various colors, first manufactured in an area of Baghdad

THE OSCAR

The first Academy Awards ceremony, held in 1927, was attended by just 250 people; now the ceremony has a worldwide audience estimated at a quarter of a billion.

The sole manufacturer of the Oscars is the Dodge Trophy Company. The original transaction in 1926 was made with the Academy by Roy Dodge, an Olympic sprinter and founder of the company.

The Oscar weighs eight pounds, is thirteen inches high, and is made of a special combination of metals, the formula of which is known only to a few people at Dodge. The statuette has a twenty-four-carat gold finish.

The first Academy Awards presentation to be broadcast was the 1928/29 ceremony, which went out on KNX radio in Los Angeles. This was also the first and last time that the awards were evenly distributed, with no picture receiving more than one award.

When the awards committee was preparing the Oscar to present to Spencer Tracy for *Captains Courageous,* they only noticed just in time that it was inscribed "To Dick Tracy."

OVARIAN CYSTS

The most bizarre of all human growths is that which occasionally occurs in a woman's ovary and is known as an ovarian cyst. Ovarian cysts are not malignant, but they can grow to large sizes unless removed.

Such growths frequently contain odd bits of skin, hair, teeth, and bones. In one case, an eighteen-year-old girl had a very large ovarian cyst that was found to contain 150 teeth, including clearly identifiable incisors, canines, and molars. In other cases, parts of a jawbone or skull have been recognized.

These growths are in fact disorganized fetuses produced by a kind of virgin birth (parthenogenesis) in a woman's ovaries. Why teeth and bone should be such a common feature of these growths is unclear.

There are even a few recorded cases of teeth developing by a similar process in men's testicles.

PACE OF LIFE

Big-city slickers walk faster than small-town dawdlers. Psychologists carried out a study in fifteen towns and cities in Europe, Asia, and North America. At each place they selected a fifty-foot stretch of pavement and timed solitary, unencumbered pedestrians over the distance on warm, sunny days.

The fastest walkers of all were in Prague's Wenceslas Square, where they notched up an average speed of six feet per second, or over four miles an hour. The inhabitants of Brooklyn weren't far behind, with a speed of five feet per second. The people of the small Greek town of Itea, on the other hand, ambled along at a leisurely two feet per second, barely more than one mile an hour.

PALINDROMES

Tongue-twisters are the word games of an oral culture, and they mean nothing in print. Palindromes, on the other hand, have to be seen to be believed.

A palindrome is a phrase or sentence that reads the same forward or backward, such as: *Madam, I'm Adam* or *Able was I ere I saw Elba*. They were invented by a Greek poet called Sotades in the third century B.C., but the first recorded example in modern times was *Lewd I did live, & evil did I dwel*, written by John Taylor (1580–1653). The acknowledged master of the palindrome was a British wordsmith, Leigh Mercer, who showed that the real skill lay in disguising the mirror image and not simply bending a sentence in half. Two of his classic palindromes were: *Sums are not set as a test on Erasmus* and *A man, a plan, a canal— Panama!*

The use of proper names is sometimes necessary, as in: *No misses ordered roses, Simon* or *Niagara, O roar again*. By using a list of reversible names, linked by a central phrase such as "sides reversed is," it is possible to build up weak palindromes of almost indefinite length, but this is cheating. The art is to make it a real sentence. For our money, one of the best is: *Did I strap red nude, red rump, also slap murdered underparts? I did!*

PENICILLIN

A twenty-one-year-old French medical student, Ernest Augustin Clement Duchesne, discovered penicillin by methodical investigation in 1896, long before Alexander Fleming rediscovered it by accident and was awarded the Nobel Prize. Duchesne tested it as an antibiotic on animals forty-five years before it was eventually tried on humans in World War II. As Charles Darwin's son remarked: "In science the credit goes to the first man who convinces the world, not to the man to whom the idea first occurs."

PERFUMES

Musk is an odoriferous brown substance produced in the sex glands of male musk deer. Women are a thousand times more sensitive to this smell than men, though this difference disappears in women whose ovaries have been removed. But since there aren't enough musk deer left in the world to be castrated in the service of the international perfume industry, natural musk has been replaced by galaxolide, a synthetic chemical that smells just like the real thing.

On the other hand, there is no known substitute for civet, a musklike perfume produced in the civet cats' anal glands, obtained by tickling their backs.

Jasmine oil also remains natural, even though it takes ten million jasmine flowers to produce just one kilo of the fragrant oil.

A number of substances used in modern perfumes are derived from turpentine. Muguol, for instance, produces a fresh lemon-flower scent, while linalool is used as a substitute for oil of rosewood.

PETROLEUM

There is no satisfactory explanation to account for the creation of petroleum.

In the 1940s, the American Petroleum Institute launched *Project 43* to find out, with six major universities studying the problem for ten years. They failed.

One rather fanciful explanation was provided in 1960 by Fritz W. Went, a Dutch-born botanist, then director of the Missouri Botanical Gardens. He proposed that the blue haze of resinous fumes given off by plants, especially sagebrush and conifers, rose high enough into the sky to be altered by ultraviolet sunlight. It was then brought back to Earth by rain and accumulated as petroleum reservoirs.

The length-to-diameter ratio of the pipe that twists an oil-drilling bit is about the same as if a dentist operated his drill with the patient at the far end of a soccer field.

PHONETICS

Standard spoken English has forty sounds: sixteen vowels and twenty-four consonants. Logic would suggest just forty ways of visualizing these sounds, but in fact we spell them in almost three hundred ways through combining our twenty-six letters. There are seventeen spellings for the long *o* sound, sixteen for the long *a* sound—thus written English is eighty-two times as hard to learn as it needs to be.

Spanish, German, Italian, and Finnish are closest to the ideal—forty characters for forty sounds.

A phonetic alphabet was installed as the official alphabet of Russia, Japan, Turkey, and Yugoslavia.

PHOSPHORUS

Phosphorus, derived from the Greek, means "light-bearing." First isolated from human urine by a Hamburg alchemist in 1670, entrepreneur Daniel Kraft bought the secret of the process and toured Europe exhibiting this new substance. A vogue developed for the medical use of phosphorus as "luminous pills" to cure all ills, and the discovery of the element in the human brain a century later led to a boom in consumption.

Its most practical use, though, was for matches. Prototypes produced in 1780 featured a wax taper with a phosphorus tip enclosed in a glass tube. Breaking the tube exposed the phosphorus to air, causing it to ignite.

Friction matches appeared in 1826, were known as "lucifers," and were first produced by John Walker, an English chemist. However, their manufacture led to workers developing an industrial disease called "phossy-jaw" in which chronic phosphorus poisoning caused decay of teeth, gums, and jawbones. England's "lucifer" industry was reformed after a crusade by the Salvation Army in the 1890s.

PIANOS

In the 1860s, an American inventor registered a patent for a piano bed; another variation on the traditional piano was one built with a curved keyboard for players with short arms.

The Boesendorfer Imperial, described as the Rolls-Royce of pianos, is nine and a half feet long and has ninety-seven keys, nine more than a traditional piano.

A young man in Paris committed suicide by lying on a bed and causing a piano to fall on him and crush his skull. The piano was balanced on a board above the bed and the man pulled a cord to tip it over onto him.

PICA

Many dogs have an oral vice that is very difficult for veterinarians to explain. Called "pica," this type of behavior makes the dog act like a vacuum cleaner, ingesting almost anything it can get into its mouth—including sticks, stones, coins, sewing machine oil, brushes, books, etc. According to vets, pica should be corrected because dogs can develop acute abdominal trouble from impacted or bowel-penetrating objects. The first step is to remotivate the animals with a large rawhide chew-toy available in most supermarkets. A muzzle can be used outdoors and is taken off only when the dog is presented with some too-hot-to-hold pebbles fresh from the oven. Pencils and sticks soaked in tabasco sauce can also be given. If all else fails, one might want to consult with a professional dog trainer who uses a radio-activated shock collar to adversely condition the dog. Vets say teething, worms, boredom, hunger, and a wide array of canine psychological problems are behind the pica habit.

PIGEONS

A municipal ordinance issued in Sienna, Italy, in 1977 said that four thousand sick pigeons must be beheaded by guillotine and then cremated in the municipal incinerator.

A German named Julius Neubronner developed a miniature camera weighing two and a half ounces, which could be carried aloft by a pigeon. The camera produced one-and-a-half-inch-square negatives, the exposures being made at half-minute intervals by an automatic timing mechanism.

At an international photographic exhibition in 1909, Neubronner sent a flock of his photographic pigeons over the exhibition hall, then quick-processed the negatives and sold enlargements to the public on the same day. A magazine of the time commented, "It is quite natural to see birds becoming photographers at the moment when men are beginning to become birds."

A survey of pigeons in Manhattan's Central Park by biology-psychology student David Fassler revealed that the birds got nervous and twitchy when they heard tape recordings of barking dogs, owl hoots, cows, college cheers, or train noises, but totally ignored the sounds of people, planes, chickens, turkeys, and volcanoes.

PLAGUES

The bubonic plague or Black Death, which killed sixty million Europeans in a series of fourteenth-century epidemics, is alive and well.

Though it no longer has the virulence it once possessed, eleven cases were reported in 1978 in America, including two deaths in Los Angeles; there have also been several deaths in Mozambique and Madagascar.

The plague is carried by fleas on prairie dogs, rabbits, deer, squirrels, and rats. Humans can be infected by a flea bite or contact with an infected animal. Initial symptoms are similar to those of flu—fever, chills, headaches, and dizziness. The disease can be cured with antibiotics if diagnosed early enough.

The locust plague is a modern as well as a biblical scourge. The problem lies in the ability of locusts to reproduce at a fantastic rate: a single male and female pair can give birth to as many as 7,500 offspring in one year. Locust swarms have been recorded that cover four hundred square miles of territory and consume eighty thousand tons of food a day.

The red locust and the migratory locust have been effectively controlled at great expense, but the desert locust defies our efforts. It may directly affect more than ten percent of the world's population.

POLLUTION

The "dead sea" is the nickname for more than twenty square miles of sewage sludge that New York and neighboring cities have been dumping into the ocean at the rate of five million cubic yards a year for more than forty years. It is now just twelve miles offshore—and getting closer.

It has been suggested that the only way to save the Acropolis from the effects of air pollution is to erect a vast plastic dome around it.

A shop in Heswall, Cheshire, England, sells bottles of Mersey Water. Its list of contents includes: "ammonia, zinc, detergent, uranium, lead, nitrogen oxide, ship bilge waste, arsenic, untreated sewage, mercury, plutonium, and a whole lot more filth."

The Mediterranean, the world's favorite swimming pool, is the most polluted sea on Earth. About one-fifth of the world's oil pollution occurs there, though the Mediterranean comprises only one percent of the global ocean surface. In addition, 120 cities pump their sewage into the "Med," ninety percent of it untreated. The great rivers feeding the Mediterranean—the Rhone, Po, and Nile—are themselves so polluted that they only contribute to the problem.

POPES

The shortest reign by a pope was that of Stephen II, who was elected on March 23, 752, and died the following day. As he was never consecrated, his name was omitted from Vatican records and given to his successor.

Forty popes have died within a year of taking office. The quickest turnover was between April, 896, and December, 897, when there were no less than six.

The longest reign was thirty-two years, by Pope Pius IX, who was elected in 1846 at the age of fifty-four.

The oldest pope was the eighty-year-old Adrian I, who was elected in 772 and lived to be 103. The youngest pope was Benedict XI, elected at the age of twelve as a political intrigue against two "antipopes"; he was reaffirmed in office twice and died at the age of twenty-five.

Twenty-six popes have been murdered.

Eighty-one of the 263 popes have been canonized, or formally admitted to the Roman Catholic list of saints. The most recent was Pius X, who reigned from 1903 to 1914. Pope John XXIII, who died in 1963, is currently a candidate for beatification, the first step toward canonization.

The last non-Italian pope was Adrian VI of Holland, elected in 1522.

When a pope dies, the Papal Secretary has to call out his original Christian name three times before he is officially declared dead. His "Fisherman's Ring," given to him at his coronation, is broken, as is his papal seal, used for documents of state. In the nineteenth century the Papal Secretary also had to tap the dead pope's head with a silver hammer.

The cardinals who elect the pope can be found guilty of their own special crime—simony, or the crime of selling their vote for money or power. In 1272, the cardinals took two years and nine months to make up their minds. In exasperation, angry Catholics sealed them up in a room until they decided—a practice that has continued ever since. The shortest election on record was in 1939, and took just one day. That was also the year when it was rumored that Hitler had sent a spy to infiltrate the election.

When Pope Paul VI attended the International Eucharist Congress in the John F. Kennedy Stadium, Pittsburgh, in 1975, he covered the quarter-mile ramp to the high altar in an electric golf cart.

Pope John Paul I, who reigned for only thirty-three days in 1978, wrote letters during the 1960s and early 1970s to historical personages including Charles Dickens, Mark Twain, Jesus Christ, Marconi, and Pinocchio. The letters were published in a religious monthly magazine when he was Cardinal Luciani, patriarch of Venice. The one to Pinocchio included the lines: "You used to watch carriages arriving in the main square and so did I. You wriggled and made faces and put your head under the bedclothes before taking a glass of nasty medicine, and so did I." Pope John Paul often said that if he hadn't become a priest, he would have liked to have been a journalist.

PRESIDENTS

President Carter sent 60,000 Christmas cards in 1977, compared to Eisenhower's 1,300 in 1956, Kennedy's 2,300, LBJ's 30,000, Nixon's 50 to 60,000 and Ford's 45,000.

Gerald Ford was the only American president to have been a male model.

Richard Nixon wore a steel-ribbed "celebrity glove" to make handshaking easier during political campaigns. According to Burke's *Royal Families of the World*, Nixon is the ninth cousin of Leka I, the exiled King of Albania.

Lyndon Johnson used to feed guests at his ranch with steaks cut into the shape of the State of Texas. He was also fond of making gifts of electric toothbrushes bearing the presidential seal. He claimed, "I know that from now until the end of their days, they will think of me first thing in the morning and last at night."

John F. Kennedy had dreadful handwriting, and it is claimed that he never signed his name the same way twice. He also had a passion for fish chowder, once eating twelve bowls at a sitting.

Kennedy suffered from Addison's disease, the symptoms of which include loss of appetite, loss of weight, and lowered resistance to infection. Paradoxically, Addison's victims always look youthful and vigorous. Kennedy was kept alive for the last fifteen years of his life by daily doses of cortisone. He also had pellets of a cortisone-based drug implanted in his thigh for his body to draw on; the pellets were renewed every three months. Cortisone treatment induces a sense of well-being approaching euphoria and a real increase in physical and sexual energy.

Harry S. Truman's favorite concoction was buttermilk laced with bourbon. The S. in his name stood for nothing and so, technically, should not be followed by a period. Rumor has it that he did not want "NMI" (for "no middle initial") stamped on his dog tags and so fabricated the middle initial.

George Washington died on the last hour of the last day of the last week of the last month of the last year of the eighteenth century.

PROBES AND SATELLITES

If the mathematicians who plotted the trajectory of the Mariner Mars probe had not allowed for the minute effect of photon pressure from the sun, the five-hundred-pound spacecraft would have been pushed twelve thousand miles off course by the end of its flight.

The danger of stress and strain in the manufacture of satellites is so critical that women are not permitted to work on delicate components during their menstrual periods; engineers dare not run the risk of subjecting their components to the extra acidity of women's skin at those times.

In 1870, a story by Boston clergyman Edward Everett Hale was serialized in a U.S. magazine. In *The Brick Man*, Hale envisaged a brick, two hundred feet in diameter, revolving around the Earth in close orbit to help navigators at sea. It was launched by spinning flywheel. Hale chose brick because he thought it would be the best material to withstand the heat of atmospheric friction.

PSYCHEDELIC

The word *psychedelic* (literally "mind-manifesting") was coined in 1957 by Humphrey Osmond, during a correspondence with Aldous Huxley, to describe the effect produced by ingesting hallucinogenic drugs. Various alternatives were proposed including: *psychehormic* (mind-rousing), *psycheplastic* (mind-molding), and *psycherhexic* (mind-bursting).

Huxley's favorite was *phanerothymic* (soul-revealing). He wrote:

To make this trivial world sublime
Take half a gram of phanerothyme.

Osmond replied:

To fathom Hell or soar angelic
Just take a pinch of psychedelic.

Ken Kesey and Abbie Hoffman both received their first tastes of LSD courtesy of U.S. Army drug experiments.

One American study asked people under the influence of LSD to estimate the sizes of various parts of their bodies. Without exception they perceived their heads as bigger and their arms as longer than normal.

Sidney Cohen, in his book *The Beyond Within: The LSD Story*, estimated that enough LSD could be carried in a two-suit valise to incapacitate temporarily the entire population of the United States.

Cary Grant once said, "LSD is a chemical, not a drug. People who take drugs are trying to escape their lives; those who take hallucinogens are looking into it."

PUBLICISTS

Russel Birdwell, one of the most expensive and colorful publicists in the history of Hollywood, was the man who launched the nationwide talent hunt to find Scarlett O'Hara for *Gone with the Wind*.

When he was hired by John Wayne to publicize *The Alamo*, he issued a 184-page document on the eve of the film's premiere in 1960—the longest film publicity document ever. By 1965, the fifteen thousand copies of it had become collector's items and were selling at fifteen dollars each.

Arthur L. Mayer, an auditor and publicist for Sam Goldfish—later Sam Goldwyn of MGM fame—once trained seventy parrots to squawk the name of Mae West's new picture, *It Ain't No Sin*. When he discovered that the title had been changed to *I'm No Angel*, he left Hollywood for New York.

PUNISHMENT AND PRISONS

The Australian aborigine ritual punishment for manslaughter is to be stabbed in the thigh by a tribal elder.

At a tribal court held in an oasis on the Gulf of Eilat, a bedouin charged with catching lobsters illegally and threatening two game reserve inspectors with his dagger was fined three camels.

A one-legged thief in Lescar, France, escaped from prison by breaking open his cell bolts with his steel false leg.

In 1974, a Federal judge in Phoenix, Arizona, dismissed as "frivolous" a suit filed by a dwarf inmate who claimed he was being discriminated against in jail. Raymond McCra, three feet eleven inches high, serving a prison term for armed robbery, claimed his civil rights were violated by the authorities' refusal to redesign his cell to suit his proportions. He claimed the sink was three feet six inches high and the shower control was out of reach.

In 1972, Robert McGregor, aged forty, filed suit in a Federal court, asking to be transferred from the Oklahoma men's state prison on the grounds that the Bible "commands man to be fruitful and multiply and replenish the earth." He said that because of his enforced sexual segregation he was unable to carry out his religious stirrings to obey God's word.

QUAKES

QUARKS, LEPTONS,
AND OTHER
STRANGE
PARTICLES

QUEEN MARY

QUEUES

QUAKES

The worst year on record for earthquakes was 1976. Major tremors in Guatemala, Italy, Russia, Indonesia, China, the Philippines, and Turkey killed at least 995,000 people and made millions homeless. The quake that annihilated the Chinese city of Tangshan on July 28th of that year was the second most destructive in history, killing 655,000 and injuring 779,000.

The most destructive quake *ever* also occurred in China, on February 2, 1556. The death toll then was 830,000.

One of the most earthquake-prone places on Earth is the Soviet republic of Tadzhikistan, a mountainous region bordering on Afghanistan. It registers an average of two thousand tremors per year, or about six every day.

Many instances of strange animal behavior before earthquakes have been recorded. Pet goldfish leapt out of their bowl before the 1976 Guatemala quake. Cattle left low-lying areas the day before the great 1964 Alaskan quake inundated their fields with a tidal wave. A woman reported that her pet turtle laid an egg, which it had never done before, several hours before a minor tremor in San Francisco in 1977, then ate it after the quake had struck. In 1975, Chinese scientists used reports of barnyard animals running in circles, rats and mice emerging from their holes, and dogs whining and barking all night, to successfully predict an earthquake near Haiching. The resulting evacuation is thought to have saved thousands of lives.

The first instrument for detecting the source of earthquakes was made in 132 A.D. by Chang Heng, a Chinese astronomer and mathematician. It consisted of a large bronze pot, around the rim of which were placed a series of dragon heads, each holding a small bronze ball in its mouth. When an earthquake struck, it would displace a heavy pendulum inside the pot, and this would in turn open one of the dragon's mouths so that the ball tumbled out and fell into the mouth of one of a series of bronze frogs positioned around the base of the pot, indicating the direction in which the quake had occurred.

One recent and devastating earthquake may have been manmade. Some scientists believe the quake that struck central Iran in 1978, destroying the city of Tabas and killing 25,000 people, was triggered by a Russian underground nuclear test that went wrong. The epicenter was unusually close to the surface, and seismologists were not allowed into the area afterward, but the feature that aroused most suspicion was the absence of detectable aftershocks. Natural earthquakes are followed by another shock about one order of magnitude less than the original, whereas underground bomb tests produce much weaker ones. Seismologists at Uppsala University recorded an unusually large Russian underground test some thirty-six hours beforehand and twenty-five hundred kilometers away, in southern Siberia.

Remco Toys once marketed "Earthquake Tower," a toy consisting of a five-foot-high cardboard tower that a child could destroy by pressing a red button, then send a rescue truck to pick up the many plastic figures that fell from the tower as it collapsed. The toy came complete with a realistic soundtrack record.

QUARKS, LEPTONS, AND OTHER STRANGE PARTICLES

What is the world made of? Atoms, of course, which in turn are made of electrons circulating around a nucleus. Split the nucleus and you have atomic power. But if you can split it, the nucleus must be made of something else again. So what is it made of?

The current theory is that all matter, including this book and yourself, is made up of two fundamental particles: leptons and quarks. Leptons are small packets of energy that cannot be divided further. There are just four of them: electrons, photons (or particles of light), and—since nature is tidy this way—their antimatter equivalents, which have opposite electric charges.

The nucleus has been more difficult to unravel. When the first atom-smashers began breaking down the nucleus, they released a bewildering number of sub-particles of all shapes and sizes. This could only be explained if the nucleus consisted of smaller units that could temporarily be arranged in different combinations, and the mathematics worked best if these hypothetical particles came in sets of three. Scientists called them "quarks," after a line from James Joyce's *Finnegans Wake*—"Three quarks for Muster Mark!"—and in order to distinguish their abstract characteristics, they called them "up," "down," and "strange."

At this point the problem seemed solved. The universe consisted of four leptons and three quarks, although scientists were slightly worried about the three quarks because one of the unwritten rules of nature seems to be that everything is symmetrical and comes in pairs.

Then the inevitable happened. New high-energy accelerators began producing sub-particles that hadn't appeared before and could only be explained by the existence of another, fourth, quark. This one was given the equally abstract name of "charm." The symmetry of four quarks and four leptons didn't last long either, because physicists were soon predicting the existence of two more quarks, which they called "truth" and "beauty."

As the number of "fundamental" particles increases, it becomes less and less likely that they are the basic structure of matter. Scientists are now speculating that the quarks themselves may be made of even smaller components—or that the subatomic particles are actually the basic units and simply go on multiplying as you put them under greater pressure, the so-called "democracy" of particles. Alternatively, in the words of physicist Dr. Allen B. Allen, "It's possible that ultimately the world is constructed from principles rather than units of matter." In other words, there is a boundary to solid reality, beyond which "things" of any sort cease to exist.

No quark has ever been separated out, and many of the sub-particles exist for such a short time that they travel no farther than the diameter of an atom. Some are beyond detection. It is a theoretical science of theoretical objects, predicted by mathematics and provable only by their side effects, although they certainly stretch the imagination.

There is, for instance, the *neutrino*, a free-wheeling lepton without mass or charge, which has so little interaction with our world that it can pass right through the Earth, or any other solid matter, as if it were no more than a faint mist. Then there is the *virtual photon*, a kind of invisible light whose main characteristic is that it can never be observed.

Some of these "particles" have more to do with astronomy than physics, like the *geon*, a particle of curved empty space proposed by Professor John Wheeler of Princeton University, and the *graviton*, a leptonlike particle of gravity which is useful for certain theories. But the strangest of all hypothetical objects is the *tachyon*, a particle that travels faster than light and *backwards in time*.

There is no theoretical objection to traveling faster than light. Einstein only showed that matter could not accelerate up to light speed in a vacuum. If the universe is symmetrical, there could well be a faster-than-light world where everything happens in reverse. The tachyon is an object which has picked up so much energy that it "jumps" the light barrier, and accelerates out of existence. It then needs enormous energy to slow down, and when it loses energy it speeds up!

There is only one place on Earth where this sort of kick could be imparted, and that is the outer atmosphere, where powerful incoming cosmic rays collide with occasional hydrogen atoms and blow them to pieces. Many scientists, including a group in Australia, are now searching the debris of these collisions for tracks of tachyons. Among the many difficulties is the fact that the tachyons, traveling backwards in time, naturally enough arrive *before* the collisions occur!

QUEEN MARY

When the *Queen Mary* was launched in 1935, her propellers were the world's largest, measuring more than twenty feet across and weighing thirty-five tons. However, they caused so much vibration in the ship's stern that, after a few voyages, they were quietly scrapped and replaced by screws of an entirely different design.

When she arrived in Long Beach, California, after being sold by Cunard in 1967 for $3.4 million, the *Queen Mary* came complete with an undiscovered cache of wine and an 1823 harpsichord in the crew's quarters.

To make the 81,000-ton liner float a quarter of an inch higher, three hundred twenty tons of paint were removed. The chips of paint removed from the ship contained traces of her wartime gray coating, and were sold for a handsome profit to nostalgia buffs by a local entrepreneur.

The former pride of the Cunard Line has been seen in many films, including *The Poseidon Adventure* and *Raise the Titanic.* She is now officially classified as a building and listed, along with the fire department and the police, as a city department. She is one of Long Beach's biggest employers, and one thousand brides a year pay to get married in her wedding chapel.

QUEUES

During their autumn migrations, spiny lobsters travel for several days across the sea floor in orderly queues of up to sixty-five animals, maintaining contact with each other by their antennae. This extraordinary behavior is apparently based on the same logic as that used in team cycling; moving in a line increases speed by reducing drag.

RABBITS

A cornered rabbit is not "hypnotized" by an attacking snake. It simply knows instinctively that the snake's weak eyes cannot distinguish a still animal from a lifeless object. Safety lies in stillness.

A publican in Bristol, England, had his hostelry guarded by an aggressive rabbit called Loopylugs. Sadly, he was kicked to death by intruders, but his son, Loopylugs Jr., has inherited his father's violent character—and his job.

An aggressive American rabbit named Harvey died in April, 1978, aged three. Adopted by the ASPCA, he was called a victim of mistreatment and became the focal point of a national campaign against animal abuse. Harvey bit sixteen people before his demise from an ear infection.

RABIES

The cure for rabies, decreed by law in eighteenth-century Ireland, was to smother the patient between two feather beds and then to get a "sufficient number of the neighbours lying on it" till he was out of danger.

RADAR

The most powerful radar beam in the world is at the Arecibo Observatory in the mountains of Puerto Rico. Its S-band radar, which has a 450,000-watt output, was used in 1974 in an attempted communication with alien intelligences in Messier 13, a globular cluster of stars some 25,000 light-years from Earth. The three-minute broadcast will take some 25,000 years to reach its destination, and it will be another 25,000 years before we get a reply—assuming that anyone is listening on Messier 13 and that any of our descendants will be around to pick up their answer. When the broadcast was made on November 16, 1974, Earth shone more brightly at the wavelength used than any star in our galaxy.

RADIO

John "Hundred-Dollar-A-Night" Massey, a popular U.S. disc jockey of the thirties, gave away a hundred dollars every night to the person whose social security number matched the serial number on the records he played.

The world's longest-running radio serial was the Australian "Blue Hill," which ran for twenty-seven years and 5,795 episodes before ending on September 30, 1976. The sole scriptwriter for all this time was Gwen Meredith, in real life Mrs. Ainsworth Harrison MBE.

In the 1920s, radio receivers were expensive. For example, the Wootophone Four Valve Cabinet receiver sold at £49 8s.; in modern dollars that's the equivalent of $1,332.

The first advertiser on Radio Luxembourg in the early 1930s was Bile Beans, a laxative.

Zaire has only four radio sets per thousand people.

RADIOACTIVITY

Three young servicemen were killed on January 2, 1961, in Idaho, in the first major nuclear reactor accident in the United States. When the core of the reactor went critical, Richard Legg and Richard McKinley died instantly. McKinley was battered against the ceiling, while John Byrnes was cut down by a flash of radiation. Their bodies were so saturated with radiation that they weren't safe for burial—in lead-lined caskets placed in lead-lined vaults—until twenty days later.

Radioactive elements, by-products of the nuclear fission process, lodge in different parts of the body for varying lengths of time. The duration times indicated are the half-lives of the elements, i.e., the time it takes for half the radioactivity to decay:

Strontium 90—28 years in teeth; Iodine 131—8 days in the thyroid gland; Radon 222—3.8 days in lungs; Plutonium 239—24,400 years in lungs; Krypton 85—10 years in lungs; Cadmium 137—30 years in muscles; Plutonium 239—24,400 years in ovaries or testes; Strontium 90—28 years; Radium 226—1,620 years; Plutonium 239—24,000 years in bones.

RATS ... AND HOW TO GET RID OF THEM

According to New Jersey chemist Dr. Gerson Ram, the best way to kill rats is to use his special-recipe biscuits. Prepare a stiff biscuit dough with .45 kilograms of white corn meal, one tablespoon of peanut butter, one tablespoon of molasses and .9 kilograms of barium sulphate. Cut into disks and bake for twenty minutes. Rats love them, but the barium sulphate sets like concrete in their intestines and they die of constipation.

A sound so shrill that it routs rats and fleas and can kill cockroaches has made Bob Brown a millionaire. He discovered the effect when building an electric guitar. He crossed some wires accidentally and noticed that rats in his basement scattered. Since that day in 1972, Bob, a guitar player crippled by polio, has built eighteen thousand rat repellent "boxes." Says Bob: "Musicians know of the overtones, the harmonics, which is what excites rock audiences, the frequencies that go through your head and you don't even know what's doing it to you. We're jamming the sensory systems of rats, cockroaches, and even ants. We've got a vibration high enough to jam 'em like a foreign broadcaster jams our radio."

RECORDS

The first sound-effects LP ever to get into the United Kingdom Top 100 was produced by the BBC Sound Effects Workshop. Called *Death and Horror*, it featured such tracks as "Head Chopped Off" and "Red Hot Poker in the Eye." According to a spokesman, all were produced by "mistreating large white cabbages."

The only known Chinese million-selling single is "Sing Along with Mao," which features the late premier chanting extracts from "little red book," *The Quotations of Chairman Mao.*

The longest word ever featured on a single is contained in "The Lone Ranger" (1977) by Quantum Jump. The word is "Taumatawhakatangihanakoauquotamateaturipukakpikimauncahoronukupokaiwhenuakitanatahu"!

The Ku Klux Klan once made a single called "Hatenanny" by Odis and the Three Bigots.

The smallest single ever made was a recording of "God Save the King" produced by HMV (His Master's Voice) in 1924. It measured just one and three-eighths inches in diameter.

The first lambswool disk was presented to New Zealand actor John Clarke, who created the popular national character Fred Dagg, for his EMI album *Fred Dagg's Greatest Hits.*

Humpin' is the title of the first LP by an Arab/Israeli band called Abu Hafla, meaning "enjoyable gathering." The band consists of a ten-piece classical Arab orchestra, three Israeli singers, a Moroccan drummer, an Egyptian tambourinist, and a blind Iraqi bongo player.

RESURRECTION SHUFFLE

A rush for lottery tickets in the town of Santa Maria Capua Vetere near Naples followed the "resurrection" in 1972 of an eighty-four-year-old butcher. He rose from his deathbed, amid wailing members of his family, eight hours after his death had been pronounced, and demanded some bread and salami.

The revival took some explaining because the death of Signor Marinetto had already been announced and relatives in America and Genoa had been informed.

The old man had been suffering from bronchitis and, two days before his supposed death, had fallen and broken a thigh bone. It was only when one of the neighbors firmly but reverently tried to close his mouth, in order to give him a severe expression in death, that he moved and then shouted for food.

The news spread quickly, and experts working the state lottery were assuring themselves of fortunes by playing combinations of such numbers as four, which was the number of candles around the bed; eighty-four, for the old man's years; forty-eight, which in the language of the lottery stands for death itself; ninety, for fear; and forty-nine, for laughter.

ROADS

Parts of the Paris-Strasbourg highway in France have a distinctly surreal air. The roadside is dotted with large geometrical plastic shapes with no apparent function: cubes and spheres, cylinders and pyramids. But the shapes are not a form of avant-garde art. They were erected in order to reduce the monotony of highway driving and reduce accidents. Spheres indicate curves in the road, pyramids and cubes a straight stretch. Red paint is used to wake drivers up when approaching a built-up area, green and blue to help drivers relax.

Roads through Russia's snow-covered northern wastes are being built out of sawdust. Prepared simply by lightly warming the surface snow and then impacting it with sawdust, the roadways are strong enough to carry heavy trucks and last for up to a year.

ROBOTS

The word *robot* was coined by the Czech playwright Karel Capek in his play *R.U.R.* in 1921. It is derived from the word *robotnik*, which is Czech for "slave."

Quasar Industries, Inc., based in Rutherford, New Jersey, has developed a seven-foot-tall robot called Sentry One, designed for guarding factories, which can chase intruders at twenty miles an hour and can then deafen them with subsonic sound waves and blind them with bright strobe lights. The company is already planning Sentry Two, which weighs half a ton, can run ten miles an hour faster, and has more sophisticated weaponry.

SAINTS

SECRETS BROKER

SEX

SHORTHAND

SIAMESE TWINS

THE SIX-MILLION-
   DOLLAR MAN

SKIN

THE SLOTH

SMELLS

SNAKES

SNUFF

SONGWRITERS

SOYA

SPACEFLIGHT

SPEECH

SPERM

SPORTS

STARS IN THEIR
   EYES

STATISTICS

STONES

STUNTS

SUBMARINES

SUCTION CUPS

SUICIDES

SUSPENDED
   ANIMATION

SWASTIKA

THE SZONDI TEST

SAINTS

According to Oxford University Press's *Index of Saints* (1978), the youngest saint was St. Rumwold, descended from the Royal House of Mercia, who died at the age of three, by which time he had professed the faith, asked for baptism and holy communion, and even preached a sermon on the Holy Trinity and the need for virtuous living.

The legend that if it rains on July 15 (St. Swithin's Day), it will rain for the next forty days, dates back to the year 971 A.D., when Swithin's body was dug up from its common grave outside Winchester Cathedral and installed in a special shrine in his honor. For the next forty days it rained solidly. However, meteorological records now show that the legend does not hold water.

St. Sabine can be invoked against gout and rheumatism, St. Apollonia against toothache, St. Benedict Joseph Labre against contagious diseases, St. Blase against sore throats, and St. Fiacre, the sixth-century Irishman, against piles.

St. Brigid of Ireland, the sixteenth-century abbess of Kildare, allegedly transformed her used bathwater into beer for visiting clerics.

SECRETS BROKER

Former CIA officer William Buchanan is the director of Carrollton's Declassified Documents Reference System, a strange publishing house that makes a business of selling recently unveiled official secrets from the files of the CIA, FBI, Pentagon, State Department, and other Federal agencies. Subscribers include the Soviet Embassy, which pays for America's old secrets with cash. Brazil, Britain, Finland, France, Iran, Norway, Switzerland, and West Germany are among other governments buying the declassified documents. Apparently U.S. officials themselves have no better way of knowing what government papers have been declassified than to subscribe to the Carrollton service.

SEX

Sex first evolved as a means of mutual repair, according to Professor Maynard Smith in *The Evolution of Sex* (1978). He writes: "If you can, imagine two simple things, millions of years ago, each one damaged in different ways, say by ultraviolet or cosmic radiation, coming together in such a way that they can cobble together one good individual. . . . Say you have two motorcars. One has the front half bashed in, the other has the back half bashed in. From the two disasters you make a good car. That's probably what sex is doing."

The idea that men's thoughts turn more readily to love in the spring may be true, but their sex hormones don't. The production of male sex hormones peaks in the autumn and winter.

Ancient Egyptian and Celtic fertility rites celebrating the sexual prowess of the ram were on the right track. The ram has a gargantuan sexual appetite and is capable of servicing as many as 40 ewes in twenty-four hours, or 365 ewes within seventeen days.

Dr. Wardell Pomeroy, one of the authors of the "Kinsey Report" of the fifties, reports in his new book, *Sexual Myths of the 1970s*, that we have merely swapped new myths for old. Among the new myths he lists are: all sexual fantasies are healthy; sex problems can now be cured by simple tricks; extraordinary sexual activity is the domain of the upper classes; sequential orgasms are best; all contemporary adolescents are promiscuous; and penis size is totally irrelevant to female pleasure.

When Cleveland, Ohio, set out to find out how its residents felt about pornography, some 280,000 questionnaires were distributed around the city by garbage collectors.

The Dani tribe of Grand Valley in New Guinea is the only known human culture that appears to take no interest in sex. Courting couples never make love before marriage, and even after marriage they refrain from intercourse for two more years. After the birth of a child, they abstain from sex for a further four to six years. The tribe has no powerful taboos or laws to enforce this lack of sexuality, and the reason for the phenomenon remains a mystery.

Chinese girls still believe that they can get pregnant by swimming in a public pool. Premarital sex is forbidden in China and masturbation is condemned as a practice that "saps the revolutionary will and excites the cerebellum." But in Canton province, prostitution still survives. Prostitutes are called "roadside chicken." Clients say the code word "motor"; if the woman answers, "son of motor," the deal is made.

Gerard Damiano, of *Deep Throat* fame, is covered by workmen's compensation should any actress become pregnant during the course of filming. Damiano also holds the distinction of having made a film called *Let My Puppets Come*, which features marionettes and hand-held puppets engaged in sex acts.

The sex film industry's equivalent of the Oscar is called the Erotica, a statuette of a "nude nubile female holding a spear."

One of the most unusual sex books ever published was *Naked Came the Stranger* by Penelope Ashe. The author was described as a demure Long Island housewife. First published in 1969, the book went on to sell ninety thousand copies in hardback and almost two million paperbacks.
It was only after the book's success that Penelope Ashe was revealed as a syndicate of twenty-five writers and editors of *Newsday* magazine, who'd written the book over a weekend to demonstrate that a trash novel could be produced and sold fast.

In order to escape prosecution, pornographic bookshops in India are called "museums."

The first school to introduce sex education into its curriculum was Abbotsholme School, in England in 1889.

The Institute for the Advanced Study of Human Sexuality in San Francisco claims to be the world's first and only graduate school of sexology, though there is systematic scholarly study under psychological and medical programs being carried out elsewhere. The Institute also claims to have the world's largest collection of sexually explicit material, some three thousand volumes and eleven thousand films and videotapes.

SHORTHAND

Shorthand is supposed to have been invented in Rome in 63 B.C., by a certain Marcus Tiro. His system contained about three thousand symbols and was so popular that it remained in use for six hundred years. It was revived by fifteenth-century German scholars, and is thought to have been used to record Martin Luther's speeches. One of the symbols of the Tiro method is still in use today throughout the western world—the ampersand sign, "&."

With modern shorthand systems like Gregg and Pitman—the latter of which uses twenty-six strokes for consonants, plus a number of dashes and dots for vowels—it is possible to write about as fast as it is possible to understand human speech, roughly 320 words per minute. Most of us speak at about 100 words a minute, a rate of about 1,500 clauses per hour.

SIAMESE TWINS

Siamese twins occur in as few as one in 200,000 births. Historical records reveal some one hundred Siamese twins born through the ages. In 945 A.D., there were the Armenian Twins, who were born joined at the abdomen and died when doctors attempted to separate them. In 1100, the Biddenden Maids, Mary and Eliza Chulkhurst, were joined at the hip and lived to the age of thirty-four. The Scottish Brothers were born near Glasgow around 1475; two people from the waist up, one person from the waist down, they lived to the age of twenty-eight under the protection of King James III of Scotland. The Hungarian Sisters, born in 1701, were joined in a similar fashion and spent their early days being exhibited throughout Europe, before being placed in a convent at the age of nine.

Joined babies were dubbed Siamese twins after Chang and Eng, born in the Kingdom of Siam (now Thailand) in 1811. Discovered in their teens by a British adventurer, they went on to travel the world, and became U.S. citizens after adopting the name Bunker.

Joined by a four-inch ligament at the base of their chests, they were of differing temperaments; Eng was quiet and cheerful while Chang was prone to fits of drunken violence. He once attacked a stranger and was saved from jail only because the judge ruled that it would be unfair for Eng to be imprisoned too.

In 1843, the twins married Sallie and Adelaide Yates, daughters of a wealthy American farmer. They fathered a total of twenty-one children in a communal bed big enough for all of them. Later their wives quarreled and went to live with their children in separate houses, while the twins commuted between the two, spending three days with each.

In 1870, Chang suffered a stroke and was paralyzed, forcing the healthy Eng to spend the next four years in bed alongside his brother. When Chang died at the age of sixty-three, Eng died three hours later because, according to their doctor, he was scared to death at finding himself attached to his dead twin.

THE SIX-MILLION-DOLLAR MAN

Popular TV series like *The Six Million Dollar Man* and *The Bionic Woman* have mixed a sharp cocktail of science and wishful thinking (for instance, the superheroes are not "bionic," they are more accurately *cyborgs*), but in one respect their protagonists are strikingly human. You may not be able to run at sixty miles an hour, but according to the American biochemist, Dr. Harold Marowitz, there is a surprising similarity.

Marowitz recently received a birthday card from his daughter, which read, "According to biochemists, the materials that make up the human body are only worth ninety-seven cents," and it set him to thinking. He decided to do some checking with the help of the catalogue of a company that supplies a multitude of biochemicals to laboratories all over the world.

First he made a list of all the ingredients that make up the human body, and then he began checking off the prices. Certain of the common items were reasonably cheap. Hemoglobin, for instance, was $1.26 a gram, and crystalline insulin cost $26.10 for the same amount.

When he reached the rarer items, the price began to rise dramatically. A substance called acetate kinase sold at $4,868 a gram, and the most expensive of all, a follicle-stimulating hormone, was a staggering $2,637,000 a gram. The amount of this hormone alone in the body was worth $13,500 at current prices.

Having finished his complex calculations, Dr. Marowitz added up the figures. To his surprise, he found that the average, non-bionic human being is worth, almost to a penny, six million dollars!

SKIN

Seventy percent of house dust consists of shed human skin, according to Dr. Raymond Clark of London's Clinical Research Centre. The human body, Dr. Clark claims, sheds some fifty thousand microscopic flakes every *minute*, and an entire layer of skin is replaced every seven to ten days. The flakes of skin are so small that they can easily pass through most forms of clothing and, before settling to the ground, are wafted up above a person's head by the column of rising hot air that surrounds the body.

A retired German army officer was admitted to the hospital with a skin infection caused by wearing his World War II medals pinned to his naked chest night and day. He said, "The pain puts me in a trance," adding that this enabled him to bear the horrors of civilian life.

Why does skin become wrinkled with age? Because the dead cells that make up the outer layer of your skin, the epidermis, are replaced more and more slowly by new cells from the layer below, the dermis. The dermis gradually shrinks and loses bulk and elasticity. Sweat and oil glands, which for years have kept your skin soft and smooth, begin to secrete less, so that your skin becomes drier and more liable to crack.

THE SLOTH

Moving through the branches at a maximum speed of one mile every four hours, comes the sloth. Grasping at branches with feet that have no soles and toes that cannot move separately, it rotates its head in almost a complete circle, looking for food and keeping watch for harpy eagles, which can swoop in and literally tear it to pieces.

The sloth has six more ribs than an elephant. It is a master of camouflage, thanks to the microscopic green algae that live in its hair and give it a greenish tinge.

It only moves when food runs out. Hardy animals, sloths can survive hunger, thirst, and injury. Some zoologists believe that the sloth only defecates when it rains, to muffle the sound when its excrement falls through the trees.

Sex occurs haphazardly, the male sniffing out the female. Both animals face each other, hanging by their hind feet. Mating takes a long time. The babies are born after a five-and-a-half-month gestation period, and automatically clutch their mother's fur so as not to fall. The mother cuts the umbilical cord with her teeth. After nine months she will reject her offspring completely.

Charles Waterton, the famous nineteenth-century naturalist, who was one of the first to observe the creature in the wild, wrote: "There is a saying amongst the Indians that when the wind blows, the sloth begins to travel. . . . This singular animal is destined by nature to be produced, to live and die in the trees . . . the sloth is as much at a loss to proceed on his journey upon a smooth and level floor, as a man would be who had to walk a mile in stilts upon a line of feather beds."

SMELLS

Dominant, aggressive rabbits have bigger scent glands and produce more complex odors than subordinate ones. The smells produced by the two classes of rabbit are so different that they can be distinguished even by a panel of human sniffers.

Dogs have been trained to detect the smell of air bubbles from the breathing apparatus of underwater frogmen as an aid in the defense of military harbors. Police in Hong Kong use specially trained rats to sniff out heroin factories.

In a laboratory experiment, human subjects were given three T-shirts to smell: one they'd worn themselves, one worn by a strange male, and the third by a strange female. The subjects were able to distinguish them with a surprisingly high degree of accuracy.

Before they fight each other, two hippopotamuses will defecate with astonishing copiousness. The animal that produces the most will usually win—apparently as a result of the morale-boosting effect of its own smell.

The female gypsy moth produces a chemical pheromone that brings males of the species flying in from miles around. The males are so sensitive to the stuff that if a gram of it were released in a single puff, they'd still be able to detect it a million years later.

On September 20, 1958, the Rhodia Company, a U.S. subsidiary of the international chemical company Rhone-

Poulenc, announced the development of a new scent film process. Since then, a number of "smellies" have been produced. In July, 1965, a Chicago movie theater showed an eleven-minute Smellovision picture that featured a number of atmospheres and smells—including that of a wet dog—all controlled by an electronic "memory drum." In 1967, the San Sebastian Film Festival featured an entry called *Catalog*, a silent film accompanied by the smells of strawberry, violet, and wintergreen.

International Flavors & Fragrances is a highly successful, highly secretive New York-based firm that specializes in artificially "creating" new and exotic fragrances and flavors. Using highly complex equipment, their flavor chemists break smells and tastes down to their component chemicals and re-create them synthetically.

IFF has produced a spruce-balsam smell for the Hall of North American Forests in the American Museum of Natural History. They've produced the smell of "salt air" in cans labeled "The Ocean" for a marine museum in Florida. A restaurateur in California got them to produce the smell of baked ham and Dutch apple, which he now sprays from aerosol cans to make his restaurant smell more enticing.

They have even produced a special bottle that produces the smell of moss, dankness, and the slight odor of bats. It's aptly labeled "Cave."

SNAKES

According to a survey involving eighty thousand British schoolchildren, the top ten most-hated animals were the snake, spider, crocodile, lion, rat, skunk, gorilla, rhino, hippo, and tiger, in that order. The snake received twenty-seven percent of the total vote.

Watch out for the python. In 1977 *alone*, two twelve-footers strangled their trainer to death in front of horrified circus spectators in Naples; an eighteen-footer that attacked a man in Indonesia was found to have the body of a forty-five-year-old man in its stomach; and a tug-of-war between a group of Indian villagers and a thirty-foot python that had half-swallowed a man ended in the death of both the snake and its victim.

In 1972, a man was restrained from entering a movie theater in Belém, Brazil, because he had a boa constrictor around his waist. Authorities said the snake was under age.

SNUFF

Lord Petersham, an eighteenth-century British nobleman, had a different snuffbox for every day of the year, depending on what clothes he wore and the state of the weather.

Every British MP is entitled to have a pinch of snuff at the House of Commons—courtesy of the British taxpayer. The snuff is kept at the entrance to the Chamber of the Commons, in an oak-and-silver box made out of the remnants of an earlier box that was destroyed during wartime bombing. The box bears a silver plate with the names of the doorkeepers who have, over the years, offered MPs snuff.

Tribes in the Amazon jungle bind two plovers' bones together to enable friends to blow snuff up each other's nostrils. So powerful are the snuffs that they're known by such names as "Leaves of the Angel of Death" and lead to violent fits of sneezing followed by vivid hallucinations.

SONGWRITERS

Actor John Howard Payne, who wrote *Home Sweet Home*, was an American expatriate. When he died, his body was exhumed from its grave in North Africa and brought back to Washington for reburial.

George Cory, who wrote the lyrics for *I Left My Heart in San Francisco*, died there in 1978 of an overdose of medication. Cory wrote the song with tunesmith Douglas Cross during a bout of homesickness while in New York in 1946. It lay unrecorded for fifteen years until Tony Bennett used it in his act at the Fairmont Hotel in 1961. Their only hit, it was adopted as the city's official anthem eight years later.

SOYA

The soya bean was first cultivated in Manchuria over three thousand years ago, but it wasn't introduced into America until the beginning of this century. The big breakthrough in soya production came with the recent development of dwarf varieties, half the normal five-foot height of the plant, which has resulted in massively increased yields. Soya is the world's most protein-rich crop.

The onward march of soya, the universal substitute food, continues apace. Already it is widely used to make artificial beef, chicken, and bacon, and now American scientists are working on a soya-based T-bone steak. "The bone is easy, just an engineering problem," said one. "The hard part is getting it to taste like a T-bone steak."

Meanwhile, a company has produced a soya milk that "has never seen the inside of a cow," and a soya product that looks and tastes remarkably like fish cake. A company spokesman claims, "It contains no fish, so obviously we cannot call it seafood. We call it 'C-food' instead."

SPACEFLIGHT

The astronaut's tool kit, designed for the first lunar landing, incorporated new devices for making repairs in the zero gravity of space. These included a Spammer (space hammer), a Plench (pliers and wrench), a Zert (zero-reaction tool), and the Nab (nut and bolt), a special wrench permitting the astronaut to apply twisting force to a bolt without moving his body.

To prepare a welcome for astronaut John Glenn, on America's first orbital flight, every light in the city of Perth, Australia, was switched on and householders spread sheets in their gardens as reflectors.

The Gemini spacecraft cabin contained seventy-five cubic feet of "free volume"—roughly equivalent to the front seat of a small foreign sports car.

NASA's BETA trainer (balanced extravehicular training aircraft), a metal saucer that floats on a cushion of compressed air and accustoms astronauts to moving about in frictionless space, is the world's lowest-flying aircraft, operating at an altitude of one thousandth of an inch. The astronaut maneuvers the trainer by means of short bursts of compressed air from a multibarreled pistol.

Black Armalcolite is a lunar mineral named after Armstrong, Aldrin, and Collins of Apollo 11, who first brought it back to Earth.

Extraordinary parallels exist between the journey in Jules Verne's *From the Earth to the Moon,* written in 1865, and the Apollo 11 moon-landing flight in 1969.
Verne's spacecraft was launched from Cape Town, Florida, a site near the present launch facility at Cape Canaveral. There were three men in his ship, which was called the *Columbiad;* there were three men in the Apollo command module, named *Columbia.*
Verne's craft traveled at about 25,000 miles an hour and reached the moon in four days and one hour. Apollo traveled at 24,000 miles an hour and made the trip in four days and six hours. Verne's astronauts ate meat and vegetables "reduced by strong hydraulic pressure to the smallest possible dimensions," while Neil Armstrong and his crew also dined partly on concentrated food capsules.
Verne himself foresaw the possibility of his fictional voyage becoming reality. He wrote, "What one man can imagine, another can do."

SPEECH

Young children prefer fast-talking adults. They like for you to speak at about one hundred seventy-five words per minute, or even two hundred if you're rushed. They do *not* like being talked to slowly. These conclusions came out of a study in which children used a machine that allowed them to regulate the speed of recorded speech without distortion. Blind children were an exception; they preferred even faster talk, at around 275 words per minute, perhaps because they suffered no visual distractions.

SPERM

In 1977 at the Royal Society in London, in a demonstration aimed to show key developments in science and technology over the previous twenty-five years, the world's oldest sperm—a 1952 frozen sample of bull sperm—was thawed in celebration of the Queen's Silver Jubilee. It was fertile.

The sperm of mice are longer than those of men, bulls, elephants, or whales. The latter all have sperm about fifty to fifty-five microns long, while mouse sperm measures around sixty-five microns. (One micron equals one millionth of an inch.)

Human sperm is unusual in being more varied in size and shape than that of almost any other species. This fact worries biologists, since variety of sperm is typically regarded as an indication of infertility—yet human fertility remains frighteningly high.

Sperm swim relatively slowly—at a maximum speed of fifty microns a second or about seven inches an hour—and in a random fashion. The idea that sperm embark on a heroic competitive swim to reach and fertilize the egg is a myth. Many sperm wriggle off in the wrong direction or change course without reason. Only about forty out of the millions of sperm ejaculated in fact reach the egg, and they do so largely as a result of minute contractions on the part of the female.

SPORTS

In 1972, an entire soccer team was arrested and put in prison in Cordoba, Argentina, after a linesman had been attacked and kicked to death during a game.

According to the World Boxing Council, 316 boxers have died from injuries received in the ring since World War II.

A boxing match held at the Miami Beach Convention Center in Florida had to be stopped by the referee when both contestants started biting each other. One of the fighters had to be taken to the hospital for a tetanus shot.

Spitting at the referee costs a professional Philippine basketball player between $66.50 and $133.

A British soccer team called the United Christian Fellowship Eleven says this prayer before every game begins: "Dear God, we commit ourselves to this game. We ask that you give us control of our minds and our mouths—particularly our mouths. Give us the strength not to swear, or be angry or violent, and preserve us from the referee."

An average British golf course requires at least 400,000 gallons of water a week to keep the greens in trim.

In the twenties and thirties, there was at least one roller hockey rink in every town in Britain. When the war came they were all converted into drill halls, and the game vanished.

According to neurosurgeon John Gleave, who spent twelve years studying which sports are most likely to cause head injuries, horseback riding came out twenty-seven times riskier than judo and forty times riskier than boxing. After boxing, in descending order of risk, come rugby, soccer, cricket, hockey, gymnastics, and track and field events.

A 1978 Gallup poll showed that forty-seven percent of all Americans now claim to do daily physical exercises. More than $65 million is spent annually on equipment such as barbells and stationary bicycles. Jogging is now so popular that nearly half of the sports shoes sold are for running. The running business alone grossed $400 million in 1978, and the whole "fitness industry" is expected to surpass $5 billion in the early eighties.

Gallup himself believes that this new enthusiasm signals a major social change. "Many behavioral and attitudinal trends in America follow the 'trickle down' process; that is, they are taken up by the affluents and are later picked up by others, and the case of exercise appears to be no different."

"We can only conclude that there is a shift in the 'collective unconscious,' " says Dr. Thadeus Kostrubala, author of *The Joy of Running*. "It's a revolution in behavior comparable to the Crusades or the inception of dental hygiene."

The tug-of-war was first recorded as a sport in ancient China.

STARS IN THEIR EYES

When the early astronauts returned to Earth, many of them claimed to have seen bright, flashing objects out in space. UFO enthusiasts seized on this as evidence of aliens, but the phenomenon turned out to be something quite different, though equally bizarre.

It is possible for subatomic particles to travel faster than light when the light itself is slowed down by passing through a gas or liquid. When this occurs, the particles produce a kind of bow-wave, like a sonic boom, called Cerenkov radiation. It was this that the astronauts saw—the Cerenkov radiation caused by cosmic ray particles traveling through the *fluid in their eyeballs*. Cosmic rays traveling from side to side looked like streaks of light, while those passing obliquely through the eye produced the effect of a shining disk.

STATISTICS

In Japan, where months have no names, but numbers instead, October 18 is National Statistics Day. A prize is awarded every year in a statistical graph competition. In 1978, it was won by a group of seven-year-olds for their study of how often mothers play with their children, entitled: "Mom, Play With Us More Often."

Dr. Joyce Brothers claims that the average American woman kisses seventy-nine men before marriage.

According to the Office of Management and Budget, the total number of hours spent by the American people filling out Federal forms in the course of a year is 784,862,000.

It has been estimated that if you were guilty of every crime shown on American TV crime shows in just one week, you would go to jail for 1,600 years.

A recent U.S. government survey—which cost $50,000—determined that the average length of a stewardess's nose is 2.6 inches.

STONES

Jade has special significance for the ancient Chinese, who believed it was the source of life and gave off masculine vibrations that could only be detected by the purest of pure women. Chinese archers used jade thumb rings to draw their bows, and it was employed as a cure for certain diseases, as a mark of nobility, and as a protection for the dead. Confucius described the "magic jade" as "firm like politeness; warm, liquid, and moist like benevolence; a pure spirit."

In a number of magical systems, quartz has the virtue of making a person invisible. The stone has to be cut in a special way and then placed for a period in tropical sunlight. The magician then takes it in his mouth and, after chanting a secret intonation, his body gradually disappears.

When the shaman of the Australian tribe, the Aranda, learns the secrets of his craft, his intestines turn into quartz crystals, which he is then able to project into people. In oriental mythology, this corresponds with the yogi achieving the "thunderbolt" or "diamond" body.

STUNTS

When French stuntman and circus performer Phillipe Petit was asked why he had walked on a tightrope suspended between the two 110-story World Trade Center towers in New York, he told reporters, "If I see three oranges, I have to juggle. And if I see two towers I have to walk." Petit had previously walked between the towers of Notre Dame Cathedral and those of the Sydney Harbour Bridge.

David Barron of Castleford, Idaho, was the first of five hundred people to jump into a six-hundred-gallon container of gooey, lime-green gelatin to search for a marble at the bottom, as a promotional stunt. Barron gurgled, "It was just like a dream I once had."

A twenty-four-year-old man attempted to jump Minnesota's forty-foot-wide Lacque Park river on a power lawnmower. He missed by thirty-five feet.

SUBMARINES

The world's first tourist submarine is being developed by the Japanese firm of Kawasaki, better known for their motorcycles. The 430-ton sub is designed to carry forty-eight passengers and to travel at depths of up to one hundred fifty feet. Tourists would look out onto the wonders of the aquatic world through the portholes of an observation lounge.

H.M.S. *Oracle* is the only submarine in active service with a crystal ball on board—a present to the captain from the compilers of *Old Moore's Almanac*.

In October, 1968, the research submarine *Alvin* sank in a mile of water off Woods Hole, Massachusetts. A year later, when it was brought to the surface, scientists discovered that an oceanographer's lunch—two jugs of soup, two apples, and several bologna sandwiches—was virtually as unspoiled as the day the *Alvin* sank. The sandwiches were soggy and the apples looked as if they were pickled, but the soup was "perfectly palatable," according to one of the researchers. Once on the surface, however, all the items rapidly spoiled, despite refrigeration.

SUCTION CUPS

Suction cups are familiar to children as part of such toys as "safe" arrows or "trick" plates that can be stuck to a table. But these cups are babies compared to the industrial version developed by a Japanese firm, IHI Industries. Three meters in diameter and capable of resisting a pull of fifty-eight metric tons, the IHI cup is designed to replace steel hawsers as a means of attaching tugboat lines to big ships.

SUICIDES

A fifty-six-year-old German, Heinz Isecke, jumped to his death from a hospital window—in order to stop himself from hiccuping. Herr Isecke had been hiccuping continuously for two years after a stomach operation—an estimated thirty-six million spasms.

A Miami woman committed suicide by drinking herself to death with water. Doctors said she had consumed so much water she could no longer breathe.

The philosopher Zeno committed suicide when he was ninety-eight because he had put his finger out of joint.

Some people like to make sure of things when they kill themselves. In a case some fifty years ago, Raymond Bloch—who was wanted by the police in an assault case—used four methods to end his life at the Belvedere Hotel in New York. To ensure success, he slashed his wrists with a razor blade, drank a bottle of disinfectant, attempted to strangle himself with a handkerchief, and then slipped below the surface of a bathtub full of water. He made it.

In a more recent case reported by the California Highway Patrol, a motorist bent on suicide rammed his car into a moving van, stabbed himself, and then was finally killed as he hurled himself under a passing beer truck.

Doctors tend to be suicidal. In Britain, women doctors are six times more likely to commit suicide than other women, while male doctors kill themselves at twice the average rate for men. The reason is thought to lie in the stress of the job combined with easy access to, and familiarity with, deadly drugs.

The most suicide-prone nation is Hungary, where forty people per 100,000 kill themselves each year. Runner-up nations like Finland and Austria have suicide rates of only about thirty per 100,000. The reasons for Hungarian self-destructiveness are obscure. The country enjoys one of the highest standards of living in Eastern Europe, and one of the least repressive regimes. Dr. Ceza Varady, director of the Institute for Mental Health in Budapest, explained: "The phenomenon reflects the Hungarian temperament, which is volatile and likes dramatic gestures."

Suicides that receive high media exposure are followed by an increase in the number of people killed in car crashes. The explanation for this curious correlation, according to sociologist David Phillips, is that a certain proportion of car crashes are in fact suicide attempts.

Between 1856 and 1857, the Xosa nation of South Africa committed mass suicide. A tribesman, Umhlakaza, experienced a vision in which the spirit of the tribe's ancestors announced that if the Xosa destroyed all their possessions, then an army of spirit warriors would rise up on an appointed day and drive the British into the sea. Belief in this vision spread among the Xosa clans like a contagion and, one after another, they slaughtered their herds of goats and cattle and burned down their granaries. But when the day came, the promised spirit army failed to appear. Several hundred thousand Xosa subsequently died of starvation in the following weeks. In the small part of Xosa territory occupied by the British, 68,000 died out of a population of 105,000. Those who survived did so only as a result of relief measures instituted by the astonished colonial authorities.

In December, 1978, shepherds in Reggio Emilia, a region of northern Italy, were baffled when about two hundred sheep drowned after they jumped one by one, like lemmings, into a fast-flowing river. No explanation could be found for their sudden mass suicide.

Sati, or *suttee* literally means "a virtuous woman," but commonly refers to the self-immolation of a Hindu widow on her husband's funeral pyre. Though banned in India during the nineteenth century, isolated cases of *sati* occurred as late as the 1940s. The practice was always supposed to be voluntary, but in certain parts of India, and especially among upper-class families, widows were placed under powerful social pressure to conform, and the life of a widow who refused was an unenviable one. A woman who did immolate herself was regarded as almost a saint. Though the origins of *sati* as a custom are uncertain, it forms part of a web of ritual suicide practices in India. Retainers burned themselves on the pyre of a beloved lord and master, as did Punjabi mothers with their dead children, so as to accompany them to the next world.

SUSPENDED ANIMATION

Embryonic mice frozen at minus 196 degrees Celsius only three days after fertilization were kept in suspended animation in liquid nitrogen for five and a half years. The embryos were then thawed and transferred to mothers by British scientists at University College, London. They were born as normal, healthy mice in 1978, the oldest mice in the world.

SWASTIKA

The word *swastika* is derived from the Sanskrit *svastika*, meaning good fortune, luck, and well-being. The hooked cross or swastika symbol is an ancient representation of the sun wheel, symbolizing eternal rebirth and movement. It first became identified with right-wing, anti-Semitic German movements as early as the 1870s, but was redesigned as the Nazi symbol in 1919–20 by Dr. Friedrich Krohn, a dentist. He first designed the symbol counterclockwise, since this was the traditional form and signified good fortune (although in its Hindu form it can be drawn in either direction), but Hitler insisted on the clockwise version.

THE SZONDI TEST

In the Szondi Personality Test, the patient is shown a series of photographs of people and asked to say which one he would prefer not to sit next to on a train journey, and which he would most like to be alone with. He is not told that the pictures are all of mentally disordered patients— sadists, paranoids, catatonic epileptics, and the like. According to psychiatrists, the choice he makes, based on his feeling of revulsion or rapport, gives important clues as to the patient's real problems.

TALISMANS
TARZANS
TELEPHONES
TESLA
THEFT
TIME
TIME CAPSULES
TOBACCO
TOILETS
TONGUE TWISTERS
TOWERS

TRAINS AND
 RAILWAYS
TRANSPLANTS
TRANSSEXUALS
TREASURE
TREES
TREPANNING
TRIBAL REMEDIES
TUNNELS
TV
TWIN SPEECH

TALISMANS

According to an old text, *Sepharial's Book of Charms and Talismans,* any person can make his own talismanic device to protect himself from evil influence, and to attract the beneficial. Through your will and your personal magnetism, you can endow any suitable material with lasting power: a jewel or stone, a vegetable or animal product, an ancient text or potent rhyme.

For temporary purposes, Sepharial states, an effective talisman can be made from a short length of new cord (new materials are always preferable, since old ones tend to be imbued with influences from past owners). First make a loose knot, then concentrate intently on the particular power (or protection or attraction) that you wish to give the talisman, and then imagine this concentrated power pouring down your arms and into the knot as you suddenly and fiercely jerk it tight. Repeat this process seven times, and your talisman is complete.

TARZANS

In the first Tarzan movie, *Tarzan of the Apes,* starring Elmo Lincoln, all of the monkeys were played by football players from the New Orleans Athletic Club, dressed in ape suits—but the lion was real.

Despite having been doped, in one scene the lion attacked Lincoln, who later recalled: "When the lion jumped me, I stabbed him and he died. After a stunned moment, we continued shooting and I stepped down on him, the remaining air in his lungs escaping with a loud whoosh. I was already shaken and you should have seen me jump."

Lincoln had borrowed the knife from a local woman who rushed off after the incident, saying, "Wait until I tell Bill tonight that I cut up the pig with a knife that had just killed a lion."

James H. Pierce, the fourth of fifteen Tarzans and the last of the silent era, was the only Tarzan to be discovered by the character's creator, Edgar Rice Burroughs. The six-foot-four Pierce played the Ape Man in a 1927 release, *Tarzan and the Golden Lion*, which featured Boris Karloff in his screen debut as a tribal chieftain.

TELEPHONES

Bigger than a Saturn V rocket, more complex than the world's most sophisticated computer, the global telephone network is the world's biggest and most intricate machine. Connected by satellites and submarine cables, the network spans the world and links some four hundred million telephones in over fifty countries, handling more than three hundred billion calls per year.

Over half of the world's phone subscribers can now communicate with each other directly and automatically without the intervention of a human operator.

Americans make 350 million calls a day on their 150 million telephones, more than 127 billion a year. Ninety-five percent of American households have phones. But U.S. studies show that almost fifty percent of residential calls are made to people within a two-mile radius.

When the telephone was first invented, people were so frightened of talking into the device that Alexander Graham Bell published a circular containing this reassurance: "Conversation can be easily carried on after slight practice and with occasional repetition of a word or a sentence."

When Bell gave the first public demonstration of the telephone at the Centennial World's Fair held in Philadelphia in 1876, the story goes that the Emperor of Brazil picked it up, listened, and exclaimed, "My God, it talks." This "fact" became enshrined in the history books—but it never actually happened. The whole incident was invented by a Brooklyn teacher in 1923 who was trying to make science more interesting for his pupils.

A physicist who filed a complaint with the Federal Communications Commission about junk calls said: "One operator, using one computer-driven dialer, could make a quarter-million calls a year. If forty machines were in use, and they soon may be, the United States would be hit with ten million junk calls annually."

The Gaelic telephone directory on the Hebridean island of Lewis is very popular because it contains the subscriber's nicknames. There are so many Murrays, Macdonalds, McLeods and the like that people find it easier to use nicknames. So Murdi Macdonald is listed as Dido, Norman Giles as Bimbo, Donald McLeod as Dolly Droggy, and Alex Murray as Eve.

Observant viewers might notice that in all American TV cop series, whenever a character gives his telephone number, it always begins with area code 555. There is no such code in real life, and this is used by filmmakers to discourage cranks who might try to dial numbers they hear on the screen.

There were many early attempts to develop broadcasting systems using the telephone. In Paris, the boulevards were lined with "theaterphones"—special booths where a caller could listen to extracts from the play at a nearby theater. In London, the "electro-phone" was a similar device that offered snatches of music. Neither system was particularly successful, but in Budapest a complete telephone broadcasting service was operated from 1893 to 1918. Its six thousand subscribers could dial hourly news bulletins, sports news, weather forecasts, and even "What the Papers Say." An added attraction was the telephone receiver's special long cord, which allowed people to use it in bed.

New York's dial-a-services include: a telephone gardener who talks to your plants, a dial-a-graduate service for employers looking for recruits, and a dial-a-tongue service for carrying on a conversation with a computer in your favorite language, and a dial-a-trivia service!

The Sentry Phone is a device developed by an electronics firm which can screen out all telephone callers except those who give a secret code. The Maid Phone, developed by Phone Services of Chicago, will place a call for you, tell you how long you've been talking, give you the time and date, count your money, and wake you up in the morning.

The world's worst wrong number was claimed by a BBC employee in London, who swears he tried to ring nearby Walthamstow and got the laundry room of the Empire State Building.

The world's biggest unpaid telephone bill was generated by more than two thousand correspondents of the world press gathered in Jerusalem for President Sadat's historic peace mission in 1977. The press center had to be installed at thirty-six hours' notice, so no billing was practical. All two hundred lines were plugged to the outside world through a cable in Marseilles.

The world's longest long-distance police emergency call occurred in 1977 when a woman living at Port Headland in western Australia was talking on the phone to her brother in Leeds, England. The brother heard strange noises and then the line went dead, so he telephoned his local police who, in turn, contacted the Port Headland police—after getting the number from international directory inquiries. They sent an officer to the sister's house just eighteen minutes later and found that the woman had been attacked.

TESLA

Yugoslav-born genius Nikola Tesla died in obscurity in 1943 at the age of eighty-seven, the owner of some seven hundred patents including that for the first electric power plant. In 1899 he discovered a way of making manmade lightning by using a copper ball atop a three-hundred-foot mast, in effect charging the whole planet with several hundred times the energy of a lightning bolt. This phenomenon created a power source that could be tapped anywhere on the globe, a fact he demonstrated by lighting two hundred of Edison's lamps at twenty-six miles distance without wires.

Tesla invented radar forty years before World War II, developed the idea of a radio-controlled rocket in the 1890s, and built the first world broadcasting station on Long Island in 1900. Tesla claimed he was in contact with extraterrestrials and told the press in 1924 that he could destroy objects 250 miles away with a ray and form a force field around the United States from twelve strategic beaming stations.

His eccentricities have, until recently, overshadowed his accomplishments. He had a germ phobia that led him to use eighteen towels after bathing, a belief that drinking whiskey would let him live to be 150, a revulsion against smooth objects, an affinity for pigeons, and a penchant for lighting lamps by subjecting his body to massive voltages. A biography, *Return of the Dove*, claimed that he was born aboard a spaceship en route from Venus to Earth in 1856.

THEFT

The Nairobi St. John's Ambulance Brigade appealed to a thief to return a life-sized human model used for teaching artificial respiration. It was stolen, along with a suitcase, from a member of the brigade while he was standing at a Nairobi bus stop.

A tall, dark, Turkish-looking gentleman walked into an electrical shop in Ilford, Essex, to buy a cassette. The proprietor, Mohammed Zamir, remembers taking a twenty-pound note from him when he asked for change and then—nothing.

Mr. Zamir recalled: "The note was a funny color so I picked it up. All of a sudden I was in a daze. Either I was hypotized or there was chloroform or something on that note."

Fifteen minutes later Zamir discovered £1,700 missing from his till.

A fifty-eight-year-old New York lawyer was charged with stealing more than fifteen thousand books from the New York Public Library, a hoard discovered by firemen who were checking the building after a fire in another apartment. The books were piled to the ceiling and covered every available inch of floor space. Stolen over a period of ten years, there were so many that it took twenty men three days to move them in seven truckloads. The books were valued at $60,000. The lawyer's only comment outside the courtroom was, "I like to read."

In 1971, an entire house—Number 10 Jardin Street, South London—was stolen brick by brick over a period of time. A police spokesman said at the time that the house had "probably now become a nice holiday home in the country or at the seaside."

A car is stolen in the United States every thirty-two seconds. This amounts to 2,700 a day, or 985,500 a year, at an annual cost of more than $4 billion to owners, insurance companies, police, and the legal system. About 50 percent of the cars are recovered, but only 14.1 percent of the cases are solved.

TIME

Pythagoras believed that time was a substance. His follower, Arhytas, defined it as a continued flux of "nows." St. Augustine once said, "What is time? If I am not asked, I know; if I am asked, I don't."

Four or five million years ago a day lasted only twenty-two hours. The lengthening of the day is due to the very gradual slowing down of Earth's rotation. Since the introduction of "coordinated universal time" as the world's standard form of time measurement in 1972, one "leap second" has been added onto the last second of each year to allow for the planet's deceleration.

TIME CAPSULES

A time capsule was buried in 1878 under Cleopatra's Needle on the Embankment in London. It included: Bibles in four languages, a box of hairpins, copies of *Bradshaw's Railway Guide of the World* and *Whittaker's Almanac*, a complete set of the coins and weights of the day, a map of London, the day's newspapers, one of the hydraulic jacks used to raise the column, a baby-feeding bottle, several toys, and pictures of a dozen pretty English women.

A time capsule buried in 1897 under a memorial stone built in Hong Kong to commemorate Queen Victoria's Diamond Jubilee was opened eighty years later. It contained coins and copies of a local newspaper, the *China Mail*, whose front-page stories quoted the latest opium-trading prices and the case of Mr. C. Holdsworth, a 230-pound Hong Kong resident who took a rickshaw driver to court for refusing his custom.

The contents of the Westinghouse time capsule buried in 1964 at the World's Fair in Flushing, Queens, New York, include: twenty million words of microfilmed text, the Bible, a piece of a heat shield from a spacecraft, a *National Geographic World Atlas* (in microfilm), freeze-dried food, a bikini, a Beatles single, a plastic heart valve, an electronic watch, a pocket radiation detector, a phial of desalted Pacific Ocean sea water, a ruby laser rod, a bottle of tranquilizers, a bottle of antibiotics, a ballpoint pen, a rechargeable flashlight, graphite from the first nuclear reactor, a container of carbon 14, a tektite mineral of possible lunar origin, film history of the USS *Nautilus*, credit cards, a transistor radio, twenty Kent filter cigarettes, a Polaroid camera, an electric toothbrush, zirconium metal, a computer memory unit, contact lenses, a ceramic magnet, a molecular block, birth-control pills, Echo II satellite material, a satellite radio receiver, a dish of pyroceram, sequoia wood, synthetic fibers, a roll of superconducting wire, fuel cells, irradiated seeds, a fiber-reinforced metal, a radiation-detecting film badge, a roll of film of Calder Hall (the world's first nuclear power station), and a plastic wrapper. The torpedo-shaped capsule rests below a granite slab with an inscription enjoining finders to leave the capsule undisturbed until five thousand years have elapsed.

TOBACCO

The first serviceable cigarette-making machine was patented by James Bonsack of Virginia in 1883, and was capable of making two hundred cigarettes per minute. Modern machines vary in rate between 450 and four thousand cigarettes per minute.

French scientists and Egyptologists studying the mummy of Ramses II discovered that among the substances used to fill out the body's abdominal cavity were tobacco leaves.

Historians had previously thought that tobacco was introduced into Europe and elsewhere by the Spaniards, who discovered the Indians of the New World smoking it. Its use for medicinal purposes—if not for smoking—now appears to have been known three thousand years earlier.

One surgeon in the team disagreed, however. Dr. Maurice Bucaille thought that the tobacco was just the remains of a cigarette that someone had dropped inside the tomb at some time since the mummy's discovery.

Nicotine is just one of some nine hundred different chemicals that compose cigarette smoke.

TOILETS

The Custer Battlefield monument in Montana has the world's first solar-powered toilet, installed at a cost of $44,400.

For water conservation during dry spells, Israel makes a toilet with a two-speed flush, delivering either three or six liters of water.

King George II of England fell to his death from a toilet seat.

University of Wisconsin psychologists Dennis Middlemist, Eric Knowles, and Charles Mather were concerned about male bathroom behavior. So in 1976 they found a small public toilet equipped with three urinals and kept a secret watch on it through a periscope. They installed devices that measured the rate of flow of urine to each of the urinals and employed confederates who would enter the toilet when one or two men were already using it. The psychologists shied away from such up-front words as "urinate" and "piss," preferring the technical word "micturate." They found that men's micturations varied in speed, volume, and length of time according to whether one, two, or all three urinals were occupied.

TONGUE TWISTERS

Tongue twisters are, of course, a traditional test of the speed of speech, and they occur in almost every language. Our own may sound comic, but when you hear them spoken in an unfamiliar language, they are almost musical.

Ken Parken, a British music examiner who has compiled an anthology of tongue twisters, considers that the most difficult one in his collection is: "The sixth sick sheik's sixth sick sheep." The length of the tongue twister is no criterion, because some of the rapidly repeated short ones are extraordinarily difficult. Try: "Gig whip, gig whip, gig whip," for instance, or: "Stop chop shops, stop chop shops." Our own award, however, goes to: "Black bug's blood, black bug's blood"—a murderous little contortion that will probably bring you to a halt in less than five seconds. Black bug's blood, black buck's blood, blag bluck's bug, back . . .

TOWERS

The New York City World Trade Center contains enough concrete to run a five-foot-wide path from New York to Washington D.C., and enough electrical wire to reach Mexico City. It has its own zip codes (10047 and 10048), twenty branch banks, food service for twenty thousand at one sitting, and when the sun shines, the gleam from the aluminum-clad towers can be seen two states away.

One Shell Plaza in Houston, the tallest building west of the Mississippi, has twenty-six elevator cabs with walls nine feet tall that are covered with real leather. The architects wanted no seams or joints, so they had to search the world until they discovered some herds of nine-foot cows in Holland and Belgium. The leather cost $1,915 per cab, or about $50,000 in all, but because of carved graffiti, the leather has to be replaced every six months.

One German couple living in Olympic Tower—Manhattan's exclusive fifty-two-story condominium office building constructed by Aristotle Onassis—sleep with parachutes under their beds in case of fire.

TRAINS AND RAILWAYS

In Victorian times, the magazine *Punch* advised all travelers to include in their luggage the *Railway Pocket Companion*, "containing a small bottle of water, a tumbler, a complete set of surgical instruments, a packet of lint, and directions for making a will."

The origins of modern steel rails go back to the "wagonways" used in English coal-mining districts as early as the sixteenth century. They consisted of parallel wooden planks along which wagons of coal could be hauled by men or horses. The first iron rails were introduced in 1767 at the Coalbrookdale iron works in Shropshire. Though their advantages rapidly became obvious, these iron rails were first manufactured not as an improvement but as a means of keeping the furnaces busy at a time when the iron industry was going through a slump.

TRANSPLANTS

The first successful muscle transplant was performed in Shanghai, China, in 1976. The patient was a young worker whose left forearm was severely injured in an accident. Part of the large pectoral muscle in the left side of his chest was transplanted to his forearm in a ten-hour operation. The patient was anesthetized throughout by a traditional Chinese herbal preparation.

The world's first testicle transplant was performed in St. Louis in 1977, when surgeons transferred one testicle from Terry Twomey (who had two) to his identical twin, Timothy (who had none). The operation made it possible for Timothy to produce sperm and be fertile. Surgeons said the operation was feasible only for identical twins.

TRANSSEXUALS

Michael/Joanna Clark is the only person ever to serve in one branch of the U.S. armed forces as a man, and in another branch as a woman. Michael Clark served in the U.S. Navy from 1957 to 1969, when he was honorably discharged. Then, in 1975, following a sex-change operation, Joanna Clark enlisted in the army reserves.

The first person ever to become a transsexual was also in the U.S. armed forces. George Jorgenson, Jr., was surgically transformed on December 1, 1952.

Colonel Amelio Robles was a hero of the 1910 Mexican revolution and had a brilliant military career spanning sixty-six years. Then he was forced to go into the hospital by a serious illness, and the doctors discovered that he was a woman. Amelia Robles, it turned out, had entered the army without going before any recruiting board when she had already given birth to a daughter, and had successfully avoided any medical examinations throughout her long career.

TREASURE

The world's largest storehouse of treasure lies beneath the warm waters of the South Atlantic. Off the coast of Florida and on the Bahamas Bank there are the wrecks of between twelve hundred and two thousand Spanish galleons, most of which were carrying large amounts of gold.

After World War II, new diving techniques allowed the search for this loot to really get under way, and it proved a lucrative business. One of the pioneer treasure hunters, Kip Wagner, began with a fifteen-dollar metal detector and eventually lifted over a million dollars worth of gold, including 1,127 gold coins he raised in a single spectacular day.

One of the most impressive finds was the *San Pedro*, which sank in 1595. In 1954, Edward Tucker and his brother-in-law, Robert Canton, salvagemen working from Bermuda, raised two thousand silver coins, jewelry, and gold bars from the wreck. This treasure included what is thought to be the most valuable single object ever recovered from the sea—an emerald-encrusted bishop's cross worth about $30,000.

Among the missing treasures of the world are a number of diamonds, including the Florentine—a 126-facet, 137-carat double rose that belonged in turn to the Dukes of Burgundy, Pope Julius II (1503–1513), the Medicis, and the Austrian royal family, from whom it was stolen in 1920—and a huge 280-carat stone called the Great Mogul, which was lost after the Siege of Delhi in 1739.

Alan Turing, the mathematician and computer pioneer, became so worried in 1940 about the possible effect of a German invasion of England on his bank balance that he invested all of his spare cash, about $666, in silver bullion bars, and buried them in different parts of the countryside. But Turing was not a very practical man, and when he went to dig up his treasure after the war, he couldn't remember where any of it was. When a friend asked why he hadn't made a map, Turing replied, "Ah, that would have been bad security."

The *Titanic* is rumored to have on board $180 million worth of gold and, in its main safe, a parcel of diamonds worth some $277 million.

TREES

If you picked a branch from a sacred tree in ancient Scandinavia, you were condemned to the following punishment; your navel was cut out and nailed to the trunk of the tree and you were then chased around the tree until your intestines were wound about it.

In 1927, a horticultural mission set out from Bombay to investigate reports of a tree that lay down at night and went to sleep. According to a description of the tree published in the *Bombay Chronicle*, it slowly inclined toward the earth after sundown, until at midnight it lay prone on the earth. It then began to rise slowly and, at dawn, was once again standing straight.

Under a decree passed in the Philippines in 1977, every able-bodied man, woman, and child over ten years of age must plant one tree every month for five years. Violation of the law results in loss of citizen's rights and a fine of up to $175. The individual gets a tree-planting certificate for each tree he or she plants. Seedlings are provided free of charge by the government, which hopes to reverse the country's deforestation by having its citizens plant some 360 million saplings per year.

The cedar and the fig are both mentioned forty-four times in the Bible, the olive thirty-seven times, the palm thirty-one, the oak twenty, and the poplar just once.

The grotesque baobab tree, found in Africa, northwest Australia, and Madagascar, is thought to be a relic of the flora of Gondwanaland, the mother continent that split up to form South America, Africa, Australia, and Antarctica. According to African folklore, when God gave every animal a tree, the hyena arrived late and received the baobab. He was so disgusted that he planted it upside down.

One hundred and twenty years after Livingstone measured an African baobab in 1853, the same tree had shrunk appreciably in girth. Because of the softness of the timber, older trees tend to become hollow, thus making it impossible to date them by counting tree rings; however, carbon dating established the age of one baobab tree near Lake Kariba to be 1,010 years old.

TREPANNING

Trepanning is the oldest operation of them all. As early as 3,000 B.C., protosurgeons could bore holes in the skull with a properly worked flint in as little as five or six minutes. One skull has been found that testifies to a man surviving six such operations.

The Incas eased the pain of the operation by chewing coca leaves and rubbing the spittle on the scalp. They then bored a series of small holes in a circle until they met, the small disks being used as amulets.

Two possible explanations for the operation have emerged. One theory holds that it was some kind of religious ritual, the other that it was used as a treatment of the mentally disturbed—on the grounds that evil spirits were locked in their heads and needed to be let out.

TRIBAL REMEDIES

It is easy to laugh at witch doctors, but much of modern medicine is based on tribal remedies. The Aztecs produced active chemicals for treating cardiovascular problems and diabetes, and long before the Spanish conquest, Indian tribes were using ipecac to combat dysentery and quinine to treat malaria.

In China today, three-quarters of all prescriptions are made up from traditional herbs. During the Vietnam war, the villagers there developed over forty new herbal treatments for complaints such as goiter, hepatitis, and rheumatism. There are 215 hospitals and fourteen thousand dispensaries across India devoted to this form of medicine, and it is still widespread throughout Central Asia, Africa, and South America.

Only about two percent of the world's wild flowers have been tested for alkaloids and other medically useful compounds, but the international drug companies have at last awakened to their potential. U.S. and Japanese firms are now actively searching for new plant sources and developing drugs from them. The Hoechst Company, for instance, has a research laboratory in India that specializes in the eight hundred listed remedies of the Ayurveda, or traditional herbalists. The Patel Institute in New Delhi recently discovered that one of these remedies contains a valuable antiasthmatic preparation and has urged the Indian government to step in before the drug companies patent it.

This raises an important moral question because, so far, none of the vast profits of the drug industry have found their way back to the people who discovered the medicines. The American Indian tribes have given the world the potato, the tomato, the peanut, quinine, the avocado, the guava, the cashew, mescaline, vanilla, chocolate, rubber, corn, and cocaine, without receiving so much as a thank you. No one has bothered to tell the Macushi Indians that curare, which they brewed originally from thirty different kinds of plant, is of major importance in modern surgery and has led to the development of neuromuscular drugs. The Ayurveda discovered the drug reserpine, but they have had no share in the vast tranquilizer business that is based on it.

TUNNELS

One of the most amazing tunnel systems ever constructed was built by the Vietcong during their wars against France and the United States. The Cu Chi network, twenty miles northwest of Saigon, stretched 150 miles, took thirty years to build by hand, and in places was constructed on three levels large enough to contain a hospital, thousands of soldiers, and even water buffalo.

According to Valentin Kaplin, safety supervisor on New York's new water route, City Tunnel 3: "There are solid rules to working in tunnels. Number one: The faster you're in and out the better. Number two: Bigger is better and more efficient. Number three: What nature hasn't built herself, she'll eventually destroy."

TV

In Japan, the national passion for TV has been called "ichioku-so-hakuchi-ka," or "one hundred million people go crazy." Ninety-five percent of the population watch it for an average of three hours and thirteen minutes a day.

In Brazil there is a TV master of cermonies called Chacrinha (Barnyard) who, for fun, throws salted codfish at his studio audience.

"Sesame Street" was such a huge hit in Pago Pago that the government considered naming the island's main street after it.

According to *Variety*, the ten movies that have achieved the highest ratings on American TV since 1961 are: 1. *Gone with the Wind*, Part one; 2. *Gone with the Wind*, Part two; 3. *Airport*; 4. *Love Story*; 5. *The Godfather Part Two*; 6. *The Poseidon Adventure*; 7. *True Grit*; 8. *The Birds*; 9. *Patton*; 10. *The Bridge on the River Kwai*.

Fifty percent of the American population gets all its news from TV.

In a survey taken among U.S. children aged four to six, when asked the question, "Which do you like better, TV or Daddy?" forty-four percent of them said they preferred TV.

"Bonanza" is one of the most widely syndicated TV series ever, with an estimated weekly audience of 250 million in eighty-five countries.

"I Love Lucy," first screened on October 15, 1951, was TV's first genuine hit, and the first TV series filmed with the three-camera technique before a live studio audience, now standard practice.

Its pulling power was such that on the occasion of the screening of Eisenhower's inauguration, only twenty-seven million watched the President's swearing-in, while forty-four million were on the other channel to see "Lucy Goes to the Hospital" for her first baby.

Fred Silverman, the wizard of U.S. TV programming, has ten rules of television known as "Freddie's Formula": 1. Make people laugh—there's enough tragedy in the world; 2. People tune in to see a star; 3. Stress the positive, not the negative; 4. The common man is more appealing; 5. It's up to me to find a new star; 6. Familiarity breeds acceptability; 7. Take chances and run scared; 8. It's not only the show but how the audience is told about the show; 9. Work the viewer's mind; 10. Cartoons aren't only for kids.

The first full-length feature film shown on American TV was *The Heart of New York*, the story of the inventors of the washing machine.

The first commercial aired on American TV was in 1941, when WNBT in New York showed an ad for Bulova watches. A watch face came on the screen while an announcer read the time—10:10 P.M. The ad cost Bulova just nine dollars.

The first TV commercial shown in Britain was an advertisement for the *Daily Mail*, which was shown at a demonstration by John Logie Baird at the National Radio Exhibition in Olympia on September 26, 1928. It was screened on a dozen sets and viewed by an audience of fifty.

The village of Carradale in Scotland has very strange TV reception. Whenever the tide goes out, the picture disappears, as if in some way the TV signal is absorbed by the mud.

In his book, *Super Spectator and the Electric Lilliputians*, author William O. Johnson claimed that the average American, living to sixty-five, spends nine years of his or her life watching television.

Television finally killed Mrs. Charlotte Gardener, eighty-eight, of London. She kept her set on twenty-four hours a day for two years until a component finally burned out and she was overcome by fumes. A neighbor told the inquest that Mrs. Gardener often phoned him at 4:00 A.M. to complain that there was no picture.

TWIN SPEECH

Two identical twins, Virginia and Grace Kennedy, have been speaking in a private language of their own for more than five years now—despite the fact that they understand English, German, and sign language.

It began when they were seventeen months old. Their mother recalls, "One would hold up an object, suggest a name for it, and the other would agree." In their new language, Virginia calls herself "Cabenga," and Grace "Poto."

Scientists call this phenomenon *idioglossia* or "twin speech." If they manage to unravel the twins' private language, they may be able to decipher the scientific riddle of whether children are born with a genetically determined brain mechanism for developing language or whether it's acquired through exposure to the spoken word.

THE ULTIMATE ANTITHEFT DEVICE

The ultimate antitheft device has been designed by Emile Kimmerle, a seventy-nine-year-old inventor, and can be used wherever money is stored or goods are on display.

Called Kim-Protege, it works day and night and can either be triggered by the thieves themselves tripping over nylon cords, or by an employee touching a button or foot lever.

Once it is triggered, panels come down on the display counter to reveal tear gas jets, which spray the thief and blind him. Simultaneously, bombs filled with knockout gas drop from the ceiling, lassos and steel ankle grips shoot out, and the thief is left trussed and unconscious, ready for the police to arrive.

If, for any reason, the thief should escape all this, he will still be sprayed with sticky red labels marked "thief," making it difficult for him to remain free for long.

UNDERGROUND AND UNDERWATER

A report from the UN Economics Commission claims living and working underground could cut energy costs by seventy-five percent.

A Russian farmhand and a milkmaid who left their work to live together in an underground "burrow" in a forest near Moscow were jailed for a year for refusing to get a job.

On London's Underground, seven out of ten passengers say "please" and "thank you," according to official figures. This compares with one out of ten in the New York subways, three out of ten in Hamburg, and five out of ten in Tokyo. The chances of a passenger's being attacked on the London Underground are six million to one.

The air in Moscow's subway stations is changed four times every hour.

The world's biggest volume of traffic in an underground railway system is Japan's, which carries five million passengers every day.

People may be able to live underwater in the future without special oxygen supplies. American and Soviet researchers have already produced a number of special materials that are permeable to selected elements.

In one Russian experiment, a hamster was able to live underwater by breathing oxygen drawn from the surrounding water through an oxygen-selective material. The development is the first step toward construction of permanent underwater habitats for humans.

UNKNOWN LONDON

Among the displays in an exhibition called *Unknown London*—a collection of plans of buildings for the nation's capital which were never built—was a scheme for a giant pyramidal mausoleum to be constructed on Primrose Hill.

The idea came from one Thomas Wilson, who, in 1824, was concerned about the acute problem of finding space to bury the dead. His solution was a pyramid large enough to contain five million corpses, which would occupy only eighteen and a half acres of ground. Made of brickwork faced with granite, it had a base as large as Russell Square, was considerably higher than St. Paul's Cathedral, and had a huge flight of stairs on every side. A central shaft would have facilitated interment, and the whole giant structure was to have had an astronomical observatory on top—all for a total cost of two and a half million pounds.

Wilson commented: " . . . the grand Mausoleum will go far towards completing the glory of London! It will rise in solemn majesty over its lofty towers to proclaim by its elevation the temporary triumph but final overthrow of Death—teaching the living to die and the dying to live forever."

UPSIDE-DOWN TEMPERATURES

We speak of temperatures rising and falling, but heat doesn't go up and down—it doesn't "go" anywhere at all. Anders Celsius, who invented the thermometer, originally numbered his scale backwards, with one hundred degrees as the freezing point of water and zero as its boiling point. Except for the accident of history that changed this after his death, we would nowadays talk of heat waves falling to very low temperatures, and be cooking at minus degrees Celsius.

Another common misconception about temperature is that hell is hotter than heaven. Sorry, but the evidence in the Bible quite clearly states the opposite. Revelations 21:8 says: " . . . the fearful, and unbelieving . . . shall have their part in the lake which burneth with fire and brimstone . . ." which means that hell must be below 444.6 degrees Celsius, the boiling point of brimstone. Any hotter and it would be vapor, not a lake.

The temperature of heaven is a bit more complicated to work out, but the clue is in Isaiah 30:26. "Moreover," it reads, "the light of the moon shall be as the light of the sun, and the light of the sun shall be sevenfold, as the light of seven days. . . ." Thus heaven receives from the moon as much radiation as we do from the sun, or fifty times in all. The light we receive from the moon is a ten-thousandth of the light we receive from the sun, so that can be ignored. Now heaven must have a stable climate if it is to last for eternity, so one can assume that the heat lost by radiation is equal to the heat gained, and heaven must lose fifty times as much heat by radiation as the Earth. Using the Stefan-Boltzman fourth-power law for radiation, and an absolute Earth-temperature of twenty-one degrees Celsius, this works out at a temperature of 525 degrees Celsius.

So heaven is about 80.4 degrees hotter than hell, glaringly bright and drenched in ultraviolet radiation. Still want to go there?

VALENTINES   VILLAINS
VAMPIRES   VISION
VEGETABLES   VOLKSWAGEN
VENTRILOQUISM   BEETLE

VALENTINES

There were two, possibly four St. Valentines. The best known was a Roman priest in the third century A.D. who was beaten and beheaded by Claudius the Goth. Two other Valentines were martyred, one in Africa and one in Rome. Relics of various St. Valentines are scattered across Europe: there is a head in Italy, a body in Rome, two bodies and a head in Spain, two bodies in Belgium, and one body in Switzerland.

No one knows how St. Valentine acquired the reputation for protecting lovers.

VAMPIRES

One of the models for the vampire concept developed by Bram Stoker in his famous novel *Dracula* (1897) was a beautiful young Hungarian noblewoman, Countess Elizabeth Bathory, who lived at the turn of the sixteenth century.

Countess Bathory's tastes ran to grotesque tortures and sexual perversions. She had a black coach in which she traveled the countryside late at night to kidnap pretty girls and take them back to her castle. After assaulting them sexually, she hung her victims by chains against the dungeon walls and slowly milked them of their blood, which she either bathed in or drank. When a girl was drained and weak, the countess finished her off by biting into her jugular vein.

Her group of weird companions included Thorko the sorcerer, Darvula the forest witch, Szentes the lesbian sadist, Ujvary the alchemist, and Ilona Joo, mistress of erotic pleasures.

Rumors of the countess's behavior led King Matthias II of Hungary to start an investigation that led to her trial. She was found guilty of murdering over 600 young women and was executed in 1614 by being walled up alive, while her companions were burned to death after being put to torture. Her crimes were considered so horrific that the trial was held in secret, and the story only became known when a Jesuit priest found the transcript in a Budapest archive.

A 68-year-old Polish immigrant to the United States, obsessed by a fear of vampires, choked to death on a garlic clove he always kept in his mouth to ward them off. The policeman who found his body reported: "There was salt everywhere. He had a sock full tied around his neck and a paper bag full on his bed. There was a bag of salt between his legs and grains on his blanket. Outside his window was a washing-up bowl containing cloves of garlic."

VEGETABLES

The "Popeye theory" that spinach makes you strong came about when a scientist at the turn of the century was measuring the vegetable's iron content. He put the decimal point in the wrong place, a mathematical error with extraordinary consequences. Spinach, in fact, contains no more or less iron than other vegetables.

Following his triumphant cultivation of the world's heaviest tomato (four and a half pounds) in 1974, English horticulturist Charlie Roberts decided to branch out. He grew an eleven-pound tomato inside a cube of clear plastic and created a square tomato ideal for sandwiches. Roberts is a believer in VIP (Very Important Plant) treatment, and plays his tomatoes a selection of radio music every day.

The world's first and only potato museum is at the International School in Brussels. It contains potato music written by Johann Sebastian Bach and informs visitors that Marie Antoinette wore potato flowers in her hat to popularize the plant.

Lettuce has been eaten by humans since at least 800 B.C. Americans eat $700 million worth of it annually.

French scientists at the National Agronomic Research Center at Versailles have grown French beans 16 inches long and one inch around. Their final aim is to produce beans as big as a loaf of French bread and weighing three and a half pounds.

VENTRILOQUISM

Ventriloquism means literally "stomach speaking" and can be traced back to the Greek oracles, whose voices are thought to have come from the attendant priests.

During the Middle Ages it was equated with witchcraft. Charles I used to have a royal ventriloquist, known as a "whisperer," who could make the sound of a sheep being slaughtered.

The art reached its peak during the days of the Victorian music hall. One performer, a Guards officer known as Coram, had a soldier doll called Jerry, who used to sit mounted on a stuffed horse in front of a view of Buckingham Palace. There was even a transvestite ventriloquist called Thora.

VILLAINS

Monk Eastman, a Brooklyn villain of the nineteenth century, cracked so many heads with his bludgeon that ambulance men renamed the accident ward of the hospital "Eastman Pavilion."

Al Capone used to be a bouncer at Coney Island. One rumor of the time was that Warners had offered him $200,000 to appear in the 1931 movie *Public Enemy*.

French gangster Jean-Charles Willoquet was arrested by members of the Anti-Gang Squad, an elite French police unit, while he was watching a program on TV about the Anti-Gang Squad.

VISION

Racing driver Stirling Moss, who was world champion in the 1950s, had such visual ability that he could allegedly change focus from one mile to twenty inches and back to one mile virtually instantaneously. One anecdote tells how Moss identified a fellow driver at such a great distance that his companion could not even be sure of the color of the car.

Twelve-year-old Sayuri Kanaka of Japan has a "third eye" on the left side of her nose. It enables her to ride her bike along a busy street or score basketball goals when blindfolded. In a carefully monitored test she was able to describe TV programs, read a story from a magazine, and catch a ball thrown to her from six yards away, even though her eyes were completely masked. Sayuri is one of the ten known cases of "skin vision"; most of the others, who are all women, can see with their fingertips. Sayuri is the first to see through her nose. There is no accepted explanation for this, but much speculation.

VOLKSWAGEN BEETLE

The Volkswagen Beetle is the best-selling car in history, outselling even the Model T Ford. It was designed in the early 1930s by Ferdinand Porsche, better known for his sports cars. When Hitler opened the Volkswagen factory in 1936, he said, with marvelous banality, "This stream-lined four-seater is a mechanical marvel. It can be bought on the installment plan for six Reichsmarks a week, including insurance."

The Beetle was first mass-produced in 1945, and since then its reliability has become legendary. Unmodified Beetles were used in the Antarctic in sub-zero conditions throughout the fifties. A Beetle half-buried in the Libyan desert for five months started again at the first try. A Beetle fitted with a propeller crossed the Strait of Messina to Sicily in thirty-eight minutes—two minutes faster than the ferry service. In the United States, a "Babies Born in Beetles Club" has over fifty members.

WALL STREET
  PROPHET
WARS AND WAR
  GAMES
WASTE
WATER, WATER
  EVERYWHERE . . .
WAVES
WEAPONS
WEATHER
WHALES

WHITE COLLAR
  CRIME
WILLS
WOLVES
WOMEN
WORDS, WORDS,
  WORDS
WORK
WORLD'S OLDEST
  SONG
WORMS

WRITERS

WALL STREET PROPHET

One of the most famous Wall Street forecasters was Frederick N. Goldsmith who claimed in 1948 that by reading a certain comic strip every day he was able to discern its hidden meaning, thanks to the spirit of a dead Wall Street speculator. Also through a medium, he was in daily touch with J. P. Morgan. He was ninety to ninety-five percent accurate, it was claimed, and subscribers paid twenty-five dollars for his newsletter. Goldsmith's annual income was $39,000, and he carried on his activities for fifty years before being stopped by the authorities.

WARS AND WAR GAMES

"Anyone may begin a war at his pleasure, but cannot so finish it."
—Niccolo Machiavelli.

Machiavelli was understating the case. Working back through history to 1496 B.C., it has been calculated that there have only been about 230 years of real peace in the civilized world in nearly thirty-five hundred years. Sometimes the wars seem impossible to stop—like the longest of all, which began between England and France in 1338 and embroiled most of Europe for the next 115 years.

Sometimes they have no end at all. There is, for instance, a phantom war still raging in the heart of Europe. Due to a clerical oversight, when the tiny duchy of Lichtenstein disbanded its army in 1868, it remained at war with Prussia, and has been so ever since.

Real wars have sometimes been triggered by games. When the Dauphin of France sent King Henry V of England a gift of tennis balls, together with a suggestion as to what he should do with them, the answer was the armed invasion of his country. In recent times the Central American countries of El Salvador and Guatemala went to war over the result of an international soccer match.

But if warfare can be a continuation of sport by other means, it also works in reverse, as in the famous incident in the front-line trenches of World War I, during Christmas of 1916, when German and British troops played soccer in no-man's-land before returning to the slaughter.

Perhaps the most extraordinary war game of all was the one that turned into reality halfway through. In 1944, the officers of the German high command were using a game to rehearse a possible attack by the Americans in the Ardennes, when news came through that the attack had actually started. General Walter Model, whose Fifth Army was involved in the fighting, calmly ordered the game to proceed, using reports from the front as his game material and transforming game decisions into operational orders for his troops.

World War II is the most popular war among war-gamers in the United States.

Chess is one of the many board games that represent warfare in miniature—especially in the Chinese version, which has soldiers for pawns and a "river" drawn across the board as a frontier between the players—but the first official war game was not invented until 1798. It was devised by Helwig, the Master of Pages to the Duke of Brunswick (presumably to keep his charges quiet), using a huge board with 1,666 squares and 120 fighting units on each side.

War games were developed to a fine art in the next century and were taken very seriously in countries with a militaristic tradition such as Germany, where they were called "kriegspiel."

When the Japanese defeated the Russians in 1904, they attributed part of their success to the assiduous practice of war-gaming.

The main contributors to the art in modern times have been Americans, especially Charles S. Roberts, who invented a game called "Tactics" in 1953, and two logistic and graphic talents, James F. Dunnigan and Redmond A.

Simonsen, who founded the first war game magazine, *Tactics and Strategy.*

WASTE

Anthropologist William L. Rathje of the University of Arizona carried out a detailed study of the garbage cans of Tucson in 1974 and estimated that in a single year the citizens threw out about ten million dollars' worth of perfectly edible food—an astonishing ninety-five hundred tons of it, including uncooked whole steaks, half-eaten apples, and over $750,000 worth of pastries. His survey showed that ten percent of the food bought by the sample families ended up in the garbage, though not unnaturally the waste was most conspicuous among middle-income families. In twenty percent of the lower-income households there was no waste, and the garbage consisted mostly of plate scrapings.

In 1975, it was estimated that there were about fifteen million junk cars in America, of which three million were rusting away in vacant lots and back yards. On the average, each of those cars contained 20 pounds of lead, 30 pounds of copper, 50 pounds of aluminum, 55 pounds of zinc, 500 pounds of cast iron, and 2,500 pounds of steel.

WATER, WATER EVERYWHERE ...

Geologists handed a report to Egypt's President Anwar Sadat in 1976, confirming the discovery of the largest subterranean water reservoir in the world under that country's western desert.

Although there is enough water in the reservoir to yield over 181.2 billion gallons per year, geologists reported that the water lies in heavily saturated sandstone, from which it would trickle at an impractically slow rate. Moreover, the water, which is said to be ages-old runoff from Chad, Sudan, and other African highlands, has such low hydrostatic pressure that even if deep wells were dug, the water would never make it to the surface.

Mexico City is built on top of a subterranean reservoir; as wells draw out more and more water, the entire city is slowly sinking.

Every year—as rain, snow, or hail—10 million gallons of water fall for every man, woman, and child in the United States.

In the human body, bones are 22 percent water, muscles 75 percent, blood serum 92 percent, saliva 99.5 percent, and tooth enamel 2 percent.

Water can be made to act as a solid by the addition of polyethylene oxide, a common ingredient of hair sprays. A student at UCLA was pouring such a mixture from one beaker to another when he noticed that the water ran *up* the side of the beaker even when it was stood upright. When enough had been poured out, it acted like a coil of rope thrown over a fence; the heavier end drags the rest over after it. A chemical reaction allowed the water to act as its own siphon!

WAVES

One wave in 23 is twice the average height. One wave in 1,175 is three times the average height. One in 300,000 is four times the average height—a killer wave, 100 feet high. Since 1969, twenty ships have been hit by giant waves, many sinking with the loss of all their crew.

Massive and majestic "waves" move through the ocean deep. Studies in the Pacific found waves at a depth of one to two miles that were six hundred miles between peaks, traveled at about one mile an hour, and sometimes took months to pass a single spot.

WEAPONS

The New York Police Department's latest arms acquisition is a bullet-proof clipboard, capable of stopping a bullet from four inches away.

David Williams, the man who invented the M-1 carbine rifle, also designed a machine gun capable of firing more than two thousand rounds a minute. Before his death in 1975, however, he abandoned work on it because he was disillusioned by the use of the M-1 as a murder weapon.

Securicor, the private security firm, varies its weaponry according to local tastes in the country it operates in. In Zambia, for instance, the company uses bows and arrows—effective because people believe them to be poison-tipped.

The International Corporation, an American arms manufacturer, has developed a submachine gun with a laser-beam sight that can see for twelve miles. The bullets are fired so fast that they follow each other one inch apart. According to the Corporation's president, W. Goff: "This gun is capable of cutting down a telephone pole, blasting through sheets of steel or through cinder block or punching through a brick wall." Three hundred U.S. police are equipped with a total of one thousand of these superguns, and twenty thousand have been sold to foreign nations.

According to the United States Alcohol, Tobacco and Firearms Bureau, almost anyone without a criminal record can buy a machine gun for around $500.

Rumanian police scientists have developed a technique for identifying individual guns by the unique profile of sound waves they emit when fired.

The most powerful gun in the world has never been fired in anger. It belongs to the High Altitude Research Project, is located in Barbados, and consists of two 16-inch naval guns welded together to form one enormous barrel 120 feet long, which can fire shells 110 miles into the air. An automatic device releases a stream of aluminized gas from the shells; this is photographed, and from the movements and distortions of the gas, wind speeds and weather forecasts can be obtained.

WEATHER

Animals can predict the weather with uncanny accuracy. Germans used to keep frogs as live barometers because they croak when the pressure falls. Ants always move to higher ground before a rainstorm, and sheep's wool uncurls.

The United States is hit by an average of 708 tornadoes a year. The worst U.S. tornado on record occurred on the afternoon of March 18, 1925. It took a three-hour, 125-mile-long excursion across Missouri, Illinois, and Indiana, and killed 689 people. In 1974, 148 tornadoes struck the Midwest in the space of just two days, killing 307 people.

Antiaircraft and rocket fire can be heard around Peking on thundery afternoons. The Chinese are trying to seed the clouds to precipitate rain in order to avoid the savage hailstorms that tend to damage crops and property in the region. Even plastic rockets and firework launchers are used.

WHALES

Since the blue whale is the largest species of animal that ever lived on Earth, and the female of the species is larger than the male, the most massive individual animal that ever existed was (or is) undoubtedly a female.

An Anglo-Saxon bestiary calls the whale "Fastitocalon" and describes it as: ". . . a deceptive floater on ocean streams, upon which men build a fire and sink to the hall of death . . ."—apparently because of sailors landing on the back of sleeping whales under the impression that they were islands.

The Arabians believed that Bahamut, a legendary whale, formed the foundation on which the world rested, and that earthquakes were caused by its movements.

Islamic legend holds that because of Jonah's three days and nights in its belly, the whale is one of only ten animals allowed into paradise.

WHITE COLLAR CRIME

The first systematic study of corporate malpractices, *White Collar Crime* by Edwin H. Sutherland (1949), defined corporate crime as the socially harmful behavior by corporations for which the law provides penalties. In his book, a study of the history of seventy of the largest manufacturing, mining, and mercantile corporations, he revealed that thirty of them were either illegal in their origin or began illegal activities immediately after their origin. Futhermore, forty-one companies were convicted in criminal courts a total of 158 times, an average of four times each.

WILLS

Mr. Ernest Digweed, a retired teacher from Portsmouth, England, left $57,957 in trust to be paid to "the Lord Jesus Christ" in the event of a Second Coming. The will states that the money should be invested for eighty years: "If during those eighty years the Lord Jesus Christ shall come to reign on Earth, then the Public Trustee, upon obtaining proof which shall satisfy them of his identity, shall pay to the Lord Jesus Christ all the property which they hold on his behalf."

The accumulated interest on the money is to go to the Crown after twenty-one years. The will further states that if Jesus doesn't show by the end of the eighty-year period, the Crown gets it all.

Mr. Halley of Memphis, Tennessee, wrote in his will: "I leave $5,000 to the nurse who removed a pink monkey from the foot of my bed, and to the cook at the hospital who removed snakes from my broth."

Mrs. Mary Kuhery of New Jersey left her husband two dollars as long as he spent half the money on a rope to hang himself.

Tom Baggs died laughing. A former war correspondent who made a fortune in advertising in America, he died at the age of eighty-four and left $99,900 to Birmingham University—to discover what makes people happy.

WOLVES

A wolf preying on calves at a state farm near Minsk, in Russia, was not deceived by tape recordings of the howling of savage dogs. But when herdsmen taped an old-fashioned tango played by a brass band, the wolf stopped dead and began baying enthusiastically. He was so mesmerized that a herdsman was able to go right up to him, throw a coat over his head, and pack him off to the zoo.

The last recorded sighting of a wild wolf in England was in 1864, but in the village of Bambridge, in Yorkshire, there is still an official wolf-scarer who is paid two pounds a year to keep the wolves at bay with a blast on his buffalo horn.

WOMEN

Women's hearing is sharper than men's, according to a study by British psychologist Diane McGuinness. Women can also tolerate brighter lights, see objects better in dim light, and are more sensitive to red and orange wavelengths of light. Men are better at reading small print.

When a Mrs. Cros of Los Angeles won a local competition for Housewife of the Year, she chose to dynamite a bridge as her prize.

A 1976 poll by the French news magazine *L'Express* found that thirty-seven percent of Frenchwomen over eighteen would rather be men.

Psychologist Gregory Nicosia segregated groups of up to eighty men or women into progressively smaller rooms. He found that men were more likely to tense their muscles, breathe more rapidly, break into a sweat, and beg to be let out of the room. These signs of stress became even more marked when conditions became so cramped that the men were touching each other. The women showed no equivalent tension or anxiety.

Out of a thousand statues in Paris, only ten are raised to women, and three of these are of Joan of Arc.

Israel's top rabbis have ruled that Jews may listen to women singing on the radio providing they don't know the woman and it isn't a love song.

WORDS, WORDS, WORDS

Groucho Marx was once asked by a London newspaper to write a two thousand word article for a fee of two hundred dollars. He turned down the offer on the grounds that he already had two hundred dollars, whereas he was not sure that he knew two thousand words.

In fact we all know a great many more than this. With 414,825 words in the Oxford English Dictionary to choose from, most of us make regular use of about eight thousand. A good journalist or novelist might have a working vocabulary of about fifteen thousand words, while Shakespeare and James Joyce are each credited with thirty thousand.

The further back one goes in history, the smaller vocabularies become. Chaucer, for instance, made do with about eight thousand words, but only the most basic peasant society could get by with a total of two thousand or less.

English is one of the most prolific languages, with roughly 200,000 words in common usage, compared with German, which has 184,000, and French, with fewer than 100,000. But although it is widely used, it is by no means the most common language in the world. Only about 320 million people speak English as a first language, whereas 550 million people speak Mandarin Chinese.

Words can be stretched—occasionally to such lengths as to become unusable.

When it comes to the longest word in the English language, most people would probably settle for that railway station in Wales—which is a hyphenated cheat *and* a proper name—or some old favorite such as "antidisestablishmentarianism." But this has only twenty-eight letters, and there is already a word in the Oxford English Dictionary with thirty—"floccinaucinihilipilification," or the act of establishing something (the word itself, for instance) as worthless.

But even that shrivels to insignificance beside the longest word of all. This monstrous mega-clump of information is the name of a protein which begins "methianyl-glutaminyl . . . " and finishes 1,913 letters later, as ". . . alanylalanylthreonilarginylserase." Fortunately, perhaps, it can be shortened to $C_{1289}H_{2051}N_{343}O_{375}S_8$, although even this requires twenty-one syllables of speech.

WORK

Susy Skates of San Francisco makes a living by distributing handbills, making deliveries, and acting as a greeter or escort—all on roller skates.

A part-time dog catcher employed by the city council in Nottinghamshire, Britain, resigned because he said there was no job satisfaction. He said the public abused him, the police weren't interested, the dogs bit him, and at £100 a year, the job was not worth it.

Laborers who apply for jobs mending Rome's tramways first have to dig a hole to show their ability.

One of the fastest-growing jobs in the United States is that of the leisure consultant, who tells you how to spend your free time.

The Labor Department's *Dictionary of Occupational Titles* now eliminates sex and age references in its list of more than three thousand job definitions and titles. So busboys are dining room attendants, governesses have become children's tutors, and repairmen are repairers. The separate listings for waiter and waitress have been replaced by one entry—waiter–waitress.

A strip-tease artist from Luneberg, Germany, applied for a job as a shepherd, claiming that at the age of forty she had become fed up with men.

Terry Colby, a beach guard, rescued eight people from drowning in high seas off Perth, Australia, then rode his bicycle to the local council offices and handed in his notice because the council persistently refused to employ an assistant for him.

WORLD'S OLDEST SONG

What is believed to be the world's oldest song, a love song or lullaby written in the Hurrian language of the ancient Uragit culture, was performed at the University of California in 1974, for the first time in 3,800 years. Ironically, although the music has been deciphered, the words themselves are largely unknown. Until the discovery of these musical texts by French archaeologists on the Syrian coast in the early 1950s, the oldest known piece of music was of Greek origin, dating from the fourth century B.C. The unearthing of the song proves that western music is about fourteen hundred years older than was previously known.

WORMS

American mathematics teacher and amateur angler Frank Kertesz has made a fortune selling cans of worms. The cans are sold to fishermen from automatic dispensers. Kertesz says his worms stay alive in their sealed cans for six months. He also sells canned leeches, flies, and other bait.

In Charles Darwin's last scientific book, *The Formation of Vegetable Mould Through the Action of Worms, with Observations on Their Habits,* there is a thirty-two-page section beginning with a discussion captioned: "Intelligence Shown by Worms in Their Manner of Plugging Up Their Burrows."

A type of marine worm has been discovered that has no mouth and absorbs food molecules directly through its skin. It is part of a unique colony of organisms, ranging from bacteria to giant clams, that live in a pocket of hot water at a depth of two kilometers near the Galapagos Islands in the South Pacific. What makes the community so unusual is that it lives on energy from inside the Earth—the heat is produced by lava excreted from the Earth's interior—rather than energy from the sun.

WRITERS

Nathaniel West died in a car crash within twenty-four hours of the death of F. Scott Fitzgerald—which was the only reason he was driving back to Los Angeles in the first place. Incidentally, in 1939, the year before he died, the combined sales of all of Fitzgerald's books totaled only 114 copies, producing royalties of thirty-three dollars.

Theodore Dreiser, in his old age, wrote to Stalin informing him that although his books were enormously popular in Russia, he had never received any royalties. He got a large check in reply.

As a baby, Samuel Johnson suffered a disease that left him half-blind and half-deaf. As a "cure," his arm was lacerated and the wound kept open until he was six.

At the age of twenty-one, Sax Rohmer (Henry Sarsfield Ward), author of the "Fu Manchu" books, was dismissed from his job at a bank for experimenting with mesmerism on his fellow clerks.

Bram Stoker, the creator of Dracula, died of syphilis.

Rex Stout, creator of the detective Nero Wolfe, invented a school banking system, the Educational Thrift Service, which he sold in four hundred towns in the United States. When war broke out, he adapted his system to the sale of War Savings Stamps and became manager of the campaign.

Nero Wolfe aside, Stout experimented with three other fictional detectives called Tecumseh Fox, Dol Bonner, and Alphabet Hicks.

Dashiell Hammett got his first promotion while a detective at Pinkerton's for catching a man who had stolen a Ferris wheel.

He wrote the last third of *The Glass Key* in one session of thirty hours straight.

Mickey Spillane was fond of relating this anecdote about his book *I, The Jury:* "Guy in Texas murdered this other feller. And on the table in the feller's home was a copy of *I, The Jury*. The murderer picked it up—and left a perfect thumbprint on the cover. The FBI checked it out and nailed him."

Western writer Zane Grey starred in an obscure 1936 Australian film, *The White Death*. It tells the story of a missionary who loses his mind after his wife and son are killed by a white shark off the Great Barrier Reef. Grey appears as a shark hunter hired to destroy the shark.

X STANDS FOR . . .   YOU WANNA BET?
ZOOS

X STANDS FOR . . .

X, as well as being the twenty-fourth letter of the alphabet, also stands for an unknown quantity, an unknown person, the number ten in Roman numerals, a symbol to indicate position (X marks the spot), or a mistake, a kiss, or a vote, a signature for someone who cannot write his own name and a symbol of films not suitable for viewing by persons under the age of eighteen.

Among the curious words listed under X in various dictionaries are the following:

Xanthippe	—shrewish woman or wife, named after Socrates' wife.
Xanthoma	—a skin disease characterized by irregular yellow patches on the neck and other parts.
Xebec	—a small three-masted Mediterranean vessel.
Xeme	—a fork-tailed gull.
Xenogolossia	—a term used in psychical research, meaning the ability to use and understand a language one has never learned.
Xerasia	—a morbid dryness of the hair.
Xenolith	—a piece of rock of one kind inside a rock of another kind.
Xenopus	—an African clawed toad used in pregnancy diagnosis, since it produces eggs when injected with urine from pregnant women.
Xiphoid	—sword-shaped. (Also *Xiphus*, meaning swordfish.)
Xoanon	—a primitive wooden image of a deity supposed to have fallen from heaven.
Xyster	—an instrument for scraping bones.
Xystus	—a covered portico used by ancient Greek athletes for exercise.

YOU WANNA BET?

New names for new things—*soap opera, Iron Curtain, astronaut*—are constantly being made up from the existing spare-parts language, but very few people can claim to have invented a new abstract word. One of these instant geniuses was a Dublin theater manager named Daly. In 1780, he accepted a bet with some friends that he could not introduce an entirely new word into common usage. The following night he went around Dublin chalking the word QUIZ on all the walls, and the following morning everyone was talking about it. No one knew what it meant, least of all Daly, and by nothing more than popular use it was adopted as a word for a joking puzzle.

Another bet, followed by some overnight work, led to one of the most famous songs of all time. In 1912, Jack Judge and a musician friend of his named Harry J. Williams were drinking with a group of actors in a bar at Saltybridge, Cheshire, England, when they were challenged to write and perform a hit song within twenty-four hours. They accepted the bet, and the following evening, on the stage of the Saltybridge Grand Theatre, Jack Judge sang *It's a Long Way to Tipperary*.

ZOOS

Wild beasts were kept in the Tower of London for centuries. Henry I had a polar bear kept there, which was let out daily on a rope to swim in the Thames. During the eighteenth century, visitors to the menagerie could either pay three halfpence or provide a dog or cat to be fed to the lions.

Henry III killed his entire zoological collection of monkeys, lions, camels, and bears with an arquebus.

The word "zoo" first appeared in a music hall song in 1867—*"Walking to the Zoo Is the O.K. Thing to Do."*

INDEX